ADVENTURES
OF A
CHICANO SPANISH TEACHER

MEXICO AND BEYOND

SONNY MORIN

Olympus Story House

Table of Contents

ForLadema and the grandkids
Holly, Adam, Caleb, Kailee, and Hunter

In memory
Jerry "Bubba" Hallstrom, rest in peace, my brother.
Thank you Gracie Peña for your encouragement.
Thanks to all who shared the journeys.

A very Special thanks to Clorinda and Carlos Torres
and my brother Adrian for your unwavering love
and support, And John Castillo and iCanConnect

Preface

"¡México es mágico!" said a random cozumeleño to me on my first visit to Cozumel. I began to believe that shortly thereafter. I love Mexico! The people, the smells, the beauty, the cuisine, and the attitude. The stories in this book cover a span of thirty-some years, twelve years after my last adventure to Palenque and four years after my last adventure to Cozumel. I traveled to Jamaica, Alaska, Peru, and Palau in between the Palenque and Cozumel visits. The book is in three parts, Palenque, Cozumel, and the other places that I mentioned. I have relied on my memory to recall all of the stories. Over the years I kept thinking that I needed to put these stories down on paper. If there was something that I was unsure of I just simply left it out. I kept the names of my buddies the same only using first names and the stories that involved high school students at the time, I changed them to avoid any legal problems in getting this book out. I begin with stories to Palenque, through Mexico and Guatemala including: Agua Azul, San Cristóbal de las Casas, Oaxaca City, Puerto Angel, Flores, and Tikal. Part two of the book includes travels to Cozumel and excursions to the mainland including: Playa del Carmen, Tulum, Chichén Itzá, and Holbox. All of these stories are true. There are no exaggerations and yes, I do believe in miracles! I did collaborate with my wife, Ladema, on our last trip to Palenque and those of my return to Cozumel, Alaska, Peru, and Palau. On my Jamaica trip I did also collaborate with my brother, Adrian, and my mother, Clorinda. I have traversed the Western Hemisphere, from Alaska to Guatemala to Peru by car, bus, train, and plane. These travels begin with those to Palenque. I hope you enjoy the stories!

PART ONE:

Palenque

1. TRIP ONE: THE PLAN

It was a couple of weeks before the spring break of 1986. My friends and I were students at Southwest Texas State University, now Texas State University in San Marcos, Texas. I was a graduate student teaching first year Spanish there. My two friends, Jerry and Randy, who along with myself wanted to do something different, go somewhere new. At that time going to the Texas coast, Padre Island, was very popular. I grew up near the beach at Corpus Christi in a small town called Alice. Growing up we used to go to the beach quite often. My mother worked for Dr. Joseph who had a beach condo in CC called the Gulfstream. We used to spend a couple of weeks there every summer. The beaches on the Texas Gulf Coast are not that pretty. I had already seen the blue waters of the Caribbean in Cozumel, Mexico, so doing the Padre thing was a non-starter.

I've always had an interest in the Indigenous peoples of the world. I started learning about the Mayan and Aztec (Mexica) peoples. I appreciated the advances of the Mayans, like inventing the concept of zero. Although they did this, they never used the wheel to build their civilizations. I saw a National Geographic show where they showcased the Mayan city state of Palenque. It was in the middle of the jungle. While visiting Cozumel on my first trip, our group went to see the small ruins of San Gervasio. It had been a place of pilgrimage for the Mayans where they had to go at least once during their lifetime. The small jungle there was nothing like the last tropical rain forest in North America.

I'm not sure where we were, but I'm pretty sure we were smoking weed. I suggested to my buddies that we should go to Palenque in

Mexico to see the ruins. Luckily neither of them wanted to do the Padre thing either, so it was set. We were going to do some trail blazing since none of us had ever done anything like that before. Being university students, we could check out some gear from the school's recreation sports department. We checked out some backpacks, the big ones with a frame and waist belt. We also checked out some trail pads, a single burner stove, and an aluminum canister for camping fuel. We were going to cook our own food once there.

I told my parents about the trip, and they were supportive just telling me to be very careful. Jerry was from Nebraska, so his folks were already far away, and I don't know if he ever told them about the endeavor. Randy, on the other hand had told his parents that he was going to Lake Amistad on the border of Texas and Mexico, for fear of them forbidding him from going on the trip. I think this prevaricaton had manifested in some way negatively.

We packed some soup packs along with canned foods which made the backpacks quite heavy. I also had a four-man tent, a sleeping bag, and a trail pad in addition to everything else. My backpack weighed about seventy-five pounds! We didn't know any better. Randy packed his prescription dive mask, thinking we might be able to dive somewhere, and a brand-new survival knife. It was nice. In addition to our heavy packs, we took a gallon of Coleman camping fuel plus a gallon canteen for water. We were getting weighed down even before we had taken one step.

Growing up in Alice, Texas, we were an hour and a half away from Laredo. My family went often to eat some good cabrito also to see me play baseball or football. It was quite safe unlike today with violence crossing the border due to the drug cartels. I have not been to the border in quite some time. Attending Texas Southmost College (TSC), now UT Brownsville, my friends and I would go over to Matamoros for lunch almost daily. No big deal. It was good and cheap. The campus was right alongside the border, a few yards from Mexico. This was going to be different; this was a real adventure. Being a Spanish teacher, I knew that I would be doing most of the talking and I was okay with that. Both Jerry and Randy had been in my first-year Spanish class at the University, so they knew some Spanish. Before I forget, we did want to go to the ruins, but what we really wanted was to go and get some *teonanacatl, "flesh of the Gods,"* mexicana psilocybe, "magic mushrooms," of which we all loved, partook and enjoyed. That being said...

Day 1

Finally, the day had come. We would be taking Randy's Jeep Cherokee to Laredo, and we would leave it in the parking garage at the Hamilton Hotel near the International Bridge. We made it to the hotel. It was already hot. We were going to take the train all the way to Chiapas. We didn't even know where the train station was. So, we left the hotel and started walking towards the border. Remember, we had these huge backpacks loaded to the max. They were heavy. We took turns carrying the water, the extra camping fuel, a gallon canteen, and a styrofoam ice chest. When we got to the bridge, the border patrol agent saw us and said, "Looks like you guys are all set to go." We all smiled and said, "Yes Sir." We filled out our tourist cards and we were off. We started to cross the bridge and when we got halfway across, I said to myself, *if this is the start and anything like this walk, then we're in for quite a trip.* I just didn't know what or how it was going to turn out. We were going "blind" so to speak.

We eventually made it across the bridge. "Whew, it was hot." Since none of us knew where the train station was, we had to ask. We asked someone and they said it was about "tres kilómetros," down the road. Three kilometers! Damn, I didn't think we were going to make it. Well, we did, but dang, these packs were so heavy. We had all this stuff and there was not a lot of space at the railroad station. So, we plopped ourselves on the floor in the corner of the waiting room. In the meantime, Jerry said that he was going to take a walk and look for something to drink. He comes back with a case of Coronas in another styrofoam ice chest! Shit, just something more to add to our "luggage." We purchased a one-way ticket to Mexico City for $9.00 U.S. on the *Primera Especial* train. The train might have been Primera Especial in the 60's or '70s, it didn't look too especial now. It would, however, serve its purpose on getting us to our destination all the way down to Chiapas. We boarded at 6:00 P.M. that evening.

2. THE TRAIN

We were on the very last car of the train and got comfortable. We didn't know how long the train would take to get to Mexico DF. We snacked some and had some sausage that someone brought along. I took some beef jerky that I bought in Three Rivers. Jerry had ground up some lab quality mushrooms in a spice container. We had some with some bread which got us ready for the evening. No one wanted to spark up a doobie since we were trying to be cautious. We settled in, made some sandwiches, and ate some sausage with some beer. Our dessert was a piece of bread with some of the mushrooms in the middle forming a bread ball, to get us through the night.

Day 2

The following morning, we were going through some canyons that were quite picturesque. We wanted to get a better view so being that we were on the last train car, we decided to go outside in the back where there was a small, gated area so that we wouldn't fall off. Randy had borrowed a camera from Clark, one of our friends back in San Marcos. It was a Nikonos V, a dive camera, very nice. We took some pictures and the train started whipping a bit and it got very shaky. It was then that Randy opened the back door and set it on what used to be a platform for a mattress. It was being used as a shelf now. I did not see him put it there. The back door had a window so that we could see to the front of the train car in case someone was coming while we were sharing a joint. We all saw a younger train conductor walk to the back of the train and turn around and walked back to the front. The conductor in charge of our train car was a nice elderly gentleman who was wearing a dark blue jacket. We didn't think anything of it until we decided to go back inside. Upon entering Randy said, "Hey man where's the camera?" "Well, where did you put it?" I asked. "Right there on the shelf." Right then, I knew what had happened. The train conductor who had walked to the back of the train had taken it. "Fuck!" So, I started to ask the people who were on our car, about twelve or thirteen people if they had seen anyone go to the back of the train. Everyone had said "No. just the younger train conductor with the white shirt." It turns out that he was the head conductor of the whole train. Some of the people we talked to, like this one elderly woman said, "It's people like that who give us Mexicans a bad name." I took everyone's name and made notes to confront the head guy.

I had to walk to the front of the train, going through maybe four or five train cars. I strapped on my survival knife to my belt, I don't know, just in case. So I walked over to where he was sitting with his family, wife and a couple of young kids. I asked him if he had seen our camera. He tried to ignore me and blow me off. I told him that I had spoken to all of the people on our car and that everyone said that he was the only one who had been to the back of the train. I told him that I had their names and testimonials. He started to sweat. He told me to have a look for myself in his mochila, his backpack. I told him that he was embarrassing himself in front of his family. I also told him that he could have hidden the camera anywhere on the train since he was the head guy. I threatened him by saying that at the next stop we were going to get the Federales to search the train. He then countered that the old man in charge of our car was going to lose his job over this and that if the Federales didn't find the camera that we would get charged up to $500 U.S. "Shit" I knew then that it was a lost cause since we couldn't take the chance since we didn't have that kind of money. "Randy, pendejo! You can't leave anything of value out of sight." He said, "They don't take your stuff in Cozumel!" "Are we in fucking Cozumel?" This was the first negative manifestation in hindsight.

Well, this was in the middle of the afternoon. It seems that we were stopping every fifteen minutes or so. People were getting on only to sell what they had, mostly food. I remember hearing a woman yelling "Atole con leche, atole con leche," oatmeal with milk. We finally made it to Mexico City at 7:00 P.M. When we got to the train station, we were all quite tired and overwhelmed. It was huge. All of the walls had schedules throughout Mexico. We weren't sure where to go next. Someone mentioned getting some seafood, so we decided to go to Veracruz, one of Mexico's port cities. We bought a one-way ticket and we had to find space on the train since most of the cars were already full. We walked towards the front of the train and found some seats. It was 8:00 P.M. when the train left. I remember a woman coming by asking if we wanted to rent a pillow for 10 cents. I gladly took one. Another woman came by selling some flautas and tacos. I asked for three flautas, she said that'll be 15 cents. I then asked for nine more and six tacos. It all came out to be a couple of dollars. By that time, we didn't even have the energy to make a sandwich for ourselves. This was the end of the second day. We traveled through the night to Veracruz.

Day 3

The following morning, we pulled into Veracruz just before 7 A.M. We grabbed all of our stuff and headed out of the station. We were looking for a hotel to shower and clean up. A few steps down the sidewalk there was sign handwritten that said "Hotel." I went in and told the person behind the desk that we only needed a room for a few hours to wash up and rest. He charged us 75 cents. We gave him a two-dollar tip. We went into the room and it was probably the right price. The shower curtain consisted of a few strips of fabric hanging with the toilet right there as well. We all showered and changed and got ready to go out on the town. After not washing for a couple of days, I was extremely grimy and dirty. We would be leaving later that evening about 10:00 P.M.

We were walking downtown when suddenly there was this rank smell. It was awful and disgusting. We were all thinking where was that funk coming from? Well, there was an old man walking in front of us. His hair was all matted long and grey and dressed in tatters. We soon went around him to get away from the smell. Jerry was taking a photography class and said that he needed a camera. He asked if I could buy him one and that he would pay me when we got back. No problema, since I had a credit card. So, we went into an electronic store and purchased one for just over $100 U.S. We needed some ice, so I sent Jerry to find some. I told him to say "hielo," like the color yellow. He came back with some. Later that evening we got our seafood and some cigars. We needed the cigars to cover up the pot smoke. When we got to the station, I had asked to purchase a ticket to Tierra Blanca since it was next on our route, according to the map of the train route that we were each given back in Nuevo Laredo. The guy said that if we went to Córdoba, we would have a shorter wait. We would arrive at 11:00 P.M. and would have to wait only one hour for the next train. So, I said OKAY. We got on the train and took off for Córdoba. We wanted to smoke, so Jerry got one of his socks and put a roll of toilet paper inside of it. We would blow the pot smoke into the sock to absorb the smell along with a couple of lit cigars to aid in covering up the smell of weed. I'm sure people could still smell it, but no one seemed to mind.

Day 4

We pulled into the Córdoba station. It was dark and not a soul was outside of the station. We walked into the station waiting room and it was packed to the max. No room for any of us, especially with all the shit we were lugging around. We decided to wait outside. It was very dark, no dogs barking or any people. We plopped ourselves on the "andén" the loading platform for the train. We figured we only had an hour or so to wait. Well 12 o'clock came and went, then 1 o'clock, 2 o'clock.

It was very difficult staying awake. We decided to take turns being on watch, since we didn't want to get jumped or beaten or anything. Three o'clock, four o'clock nothing. Finally at five o'clock a train pulled into the station, and everyone started pouring out of the station. We hurried too since we didn't want to be standing for the whole trip heading further south. Well Randy was so tired he grabbed his backpack and put it on the rack above his seat and plopped himself down to sleep. Jerry and I on the other hand wanted to get comfortable and un-bungied our sleeping bags to cover up. The train started to pull out of the station. Something told me to ask the woman sitting in front of me, where the train was going? We didn't know for sure. So, I ask the woman, "Señora, ¿Adónde va este tren?" She said "Mejico," meaning Mexico City. "FUUUCK!" We were on the wrong train!! Randy was out like a rock. I went over to him, yelling and shaking him, "Randy! Randy! Wake the fuck up!!! We're on the wrong train!!" No response, so I slapped the shit out of him. "HEY! What the fuck!" he yelled. I yelled back, "We're on the wrong train we have to get off now!" The train was starting to pick up speed. He grabbed his backpack and one of the ice chests and jumped off. Jerry and I on the other hand, had to bungy our sleeping bags to our backpacks, grab everything else, and then we jumped off. We saw another train pull into the station across the train yard. The ground was rocky and uneven. Remember it was five in the morning and still dark. As we ran towards the train that was pulling in, I tripped and fell and the styrofoam ice chest that I was carrying exploded on impact. All of a sudden, there are all these kids picking up the contents of the ice chest as if it were a piñata. Randy saw the trouble that we were having and set his backpack on the train and was running to help us. I yelled at him to get back on the train, since it was starting to pull out. Jerry and I were running to get on the back part of the train where Randy was. Now, that the train was pulling out, we were running to get on the engine car at the front part of the train. Jerry is a big guy. He was able to run and jump on the engine car. I, on the other hand, not a big guy. As I was running, I was removing and trying to hand him my heavy ass backpack. He was able to grab it while I was trying to get my footing anywhere possible, so that I could pull myself up. Unfortunately, my foot slipped off a piece of metal and my weight carried me under the train. Jerry sees me fall underneath and immediately jumps off to see if I was okay. When I fell underneath, I came face to face with the train wheel, so I made myself as skinny as I could and rolled away from it. Jerry asked, "Are you okay?" "Yeah," I said, but, "Oh well there goes Randy."

Apparently, there was an old man seeing all this unfold. He must have been laughing his ass off at us. He came over to us saying that the train was only pulling up to back up to the train platform. When the train stopped, Randy jumped out and asked us, "Hey man where's my backpack?" "I don't know, where did you put it?" Come to find out, Córdoba was notorious for bandits ripping off people. Finally, we got on the right train heading in the right direction. Randy was pissed. He said, "Well hell, we might as well go back home." Jerry and I looked at each other and said "No, we didn't come this far for nothing." We piled all of our stuff in the front of the train where Randy laid on top of everything, saying, "Nobody's gonna get these." In hindsight, was this another negative manifestation of the lie Randy had told his parents? Hmmm, who knows.

This was the fourth day into our adventure. At 8 A.M. later that morning, the train came to a complete stop. There was another train on the same track as our train heading in the opposite direction. We had to wait about an hour and a half to allow the other train to back up. We proceeded when at 11 A.M. there was a big crash that jolted and shook the whole train. We looked out the window and there was all this black stuff that covered the grass outside. The train had hit a tanker truck carrying hot tar. There were some children who got covered in the tar. A Corona truck was used to transport them. I think one of the kids might have gotten hurt. I sure hope they were all okay. We were stranded until about three o'clock. We pulled into Coatzalcoalcos or Aguascalientes, I'm not sure, for a short layover. We went looking for a doctor's office or pharmacy, trying to get some Valium. Randy said that he would go in and talk to the doctor. We rehearsed what he would say. I told him how to say that he was robbed and was in a train crash. He was going to tell what had happened. We all looked kind of rough and a little down and out. Randy had a stupid look about him. His hair was messed up and all. It was hilarious. While he didn't get the Valium, he did get something to help him sleep. We all could use the rest. Let me just mention that once on a Cozumel trip it was the same situation. Randy had wanted to get some Valium or something. We drove to the hospital there in Cozumel. He goes in and comes back out. Turns out, they wouldn't give him anything, except a shot of some kind. Yes, he got an injection at the hospital. It was hilarious!

We got back on the train and made sure it was the right one. After about thirty minutes or so, we went out to the back part of the train outside to smoke some weed to help take the edge off. The train conductor came out to where we were, and I had the doobie over the gate trying to hide it. The conductor grabbed my arm and pulled it up toward his mouth and took a hit off the joint! "Buena mota" he said. Good weed. I told him that we were trying to score some. He asked, "Didn't you see them selling it right by the train at our last stop?" No shit? He said that we would probably find some more on the way. He was a cool guy, unlike the asshole who stole our camera. It's funny how pot smokers always seem to find each other. I don't know what it is, but we do. He gave me a joint holder that looked like a little natural horn that came from a tree or woody plant or something. It's all about the journey, as they say, always interesting and constantly changing. We traveled throughout the night to get to Palenque. It has already been quite adventurous. No telling what awaits us.

3. PALENQUE, MAYABELL, AND THE RUINS

Day 5

At last, on the morning of our fifth day, we were pulling into the Palenque station. It was eight kilometers from the small town of Palenque! So, we walked the whole way. Now Randy didn't have his backpack to carry so he was designated to carry everything else. Neither Jerry, nor I, wanted him to carry our stuff. We made the long ass walk from the station to Palenque. Coming into town, there was a huge white Mayan head statue. We all looked in amazement. We've finally made it. We were happy and our quest to get some shrooms began. We walked down the main dusty street all the way down where there was a little park or plaza with trees. We started asking around where could we find some mushrooms? This one guy said, "At the ruins," which was where we were going anyway. We had a quick breakfast with a view of the jungle through a restaurant window. We each also bought a blanket since we hadn't brought one. We took a colectivo, a small van to the archaeological zone. The driver dropped us off at the Mayabell campground. There was a small white sign with painted black letters, MAYABELL.

We made our way in. At the entrance on the left, was a big Ceiba tree. As we walked further into the campground, we smelled that smell and felt we were home! They told us to find a palapa and that someone would stop by later to collect our lodging fees. It was very laid back. We found an empty palapa on the right edge of the campground. Next to our palapa was a couple with their young son, maybe four or five years old. In another palapa nearby we met Chris Ubmann, a forestry worker from Switzerland. He was a real nice guy who took a liking to us. We would end up sending post cards to each other a couple of years after. Well, he educated us giving us the lowdown of the area. We told him that we were here for only two or three nights which blew him away. Having come so far for such a short period of time was hard for him to believe. He had already been traveling through Mexico for a month and had another month to go. In la Suiza, he said everyone has two months paid mandatory vacation, and that he was learning Spanish by talking to kids along the way. He was a nice guy; clean cut and he wore glasses.

I set up my tent in which I slept for the first night. It was too hot for me. I later slept in the cheap hammock that I bought at Wal-Mart back in San Marcos. Well, the guy that worked there came by and picked up our $1.00 each for the night. We were getting hungry and decided to start preparing some soup. We used the single-burner stove for the soup. I also wanted to make a small fire and gathered some firewood. Being in the jungle, wood is usually damp. It didn't seem to want to catch. I thought that maybe I could spark it up with some lantern fuel. I thought about pouring small amount in the cap of the fuel can. The fuel is like gasoline, I knew that. But I couldn't be bothered. I figured I could just jerk some fuel out of the can quickly with no problem. *WRONG!* As soon as I jerked some out towards the little flame it, the flame followed back to the fuel can and fire was coming out. Shit! As I'm holding the fuel can I threw it away from the palapa, fire and fuel poured out creating a wall of fire. It lit up the jungle, there was fire everywhere. I yelled for Chris, "Hey do something!" He yelled back, "I fly in a helicopter." The fire started to burn out in a short time. Everything in the jungle is just so green. I moved the fuel can to where I was able to get the cap back on and put it out. Shit, What the fuck else can happen? We ate and were tired. I slept in the tent, which for me, was way too hot. But it gets cold in the jungle at night. I guess Randy and Jerry got cold. One of them switched out with me the following night. Later that evening the howler monkeys started to roar. It sounded almost like a lion. You could hear some in the far distance, but there were some nearby as well. It was loud.

Day 6

New day. We got up excited knowing that we would be going to the ruins. They were about a mile down the road. Walking without our backpacks was a piece of cake. We all took turns carrying the one-gallon canteen. As we got closer to the ruins on the left was a jungle trail leading to the back part of the ruins, somewhat of a back entrance that was free. Across the road from the back path was what looked like a closed down hotel. It looked like it could have been a happening place at one time. Along the muddy trail was like a small stream or river. We walked and climbed over tree roots pulling ourselves up trying not to slip and fall. We saw what was the "Queens Bath." A small natural pool area with waterfalls. We took note and decided to wait until we made our way back out. We would cool off later.

We finally made it to the top of the hill and began walking towards the interior of the park. We saw all these temples, the Palace, the Tower, and the Temple of the Inscriptions. We were blown away. It was an amazing feeling, walking around and in kind of a dream-like state. Back then we were allowed to climb up the Tower and the Temple of Inscriptions. That's where Alberto Ruz, the archaeologist who found King Pacal back in the 1940s. It took him seven seasons to finally dig out the stairway leading to the bottom of the tomb inside. Ruz is buried there in front of the Temple of Inscriptions in a small tomb. We climbed up the pyramid steps in a zig-zag pattern so that more of our foot would stay on the narrow steps to the top. We were exhausted when we got to the top. Inside of the Temple of Inscriptions was a bas-relief carving on the back wall. To the left, was the staircase leading down to the tomb of Pacal.

We made our way down the damp ziggity-zaggity stairway down to the tomb. We were the only ones down there. We made it to the bottom and saw the triangle shaped door. It had vertical metal bars and was locked. Through the door we saw the sarcophagus where King Pacal was buried with his famous jade mask, which I would see years later in the National Museum of Anthropology near Chapultepec Park in Mexico City. We took some pictures with the gate in the background. We went back up, ready to explore some more. Before we headed down the Temple of Inscriptions, we decided to take some more pictures from on top of the Temple. Jerry took one from the top right corner looking at the only tower in the Mayan world that I know of. I later enlarged the picture to a 20 by 30 poster and still have it hanging in the den over my computer where I'm writing this. Well, we decided to walk to the backside of the Temple to spark up. We made sure there was no one around. Just sitting there on the back part of the Temple looking at the jungle was an awesome feeling. I just kept thinking how damn lucky I was, being able to have that experience.

We made our way down the pyramid, and we were just about out of water. We walked around and saw a small spring fed stream that led into an ancient aqueduct. The water was clear and looked very clean. I cupped some water in my hand and drank. It was freaking great. The guys thought the same, so I decided to fill up the canteen. None of us ever got sick. It was good water. You hear stories about not drinking the water or else get ready for Moctezuma's revenge. We walked around the Palace Complex and climbed up the narrow staircase to the top of the Tower. Back in ancient times, the Mayans would light a fire every 52 years to make sure the world would keep on keeping on. Well again, we just had to spark up another one and just take in the view. We spent probably an hour up on the Tower, just us three. It was already later in the afternoon, and we were ready to cool off. We exited from where we entered and decided to go for a swim. I stepped in the pool to test the water and with my first step I plunged all the way down over my head. Whoosh, I didn't expect that. The water felt great and refreshing and it was very scenic, and we took more pics, eventually we made our way out of the jungle and back to Mayabell.

Back at hippie central, Mayabell, we made some more soup. At Mayabell there was a small restaurant and hot showers too. As I was laying in my hammock, I saw a kid chasing something through the tall grass with his machete. I yelled at him, "Hey what are you doing?" "Getting lunch," he said. He picked up a large gray knocked out iguana. I asked him, "Does it taste like chicken?" "Yeah," he said. Later, we ate, and I think Jerry had taken a walk to the restaurant and came back with some rice which we added to the soup along with some "special herbs and spices," ground up mushrooms that Jerry brought. We were going out first thing in the morning to look for some. I slept in the hammock which was much cooler than sleeping in the tent. I just covered up with a blanket and stayed warm.

4. Walkabout, the Search, the Big Tree

Day 7

We headed out early in the morning walking towards the ruins. We had been told to go out towards the dirt road just past the old hotel across from the back entrance to the ruins. We walked down the road a way and were soon met by a farmer. We talked and he already knew what we were looking for. He said, "Let's take a walk." We headed down the road and it began to incline up small hill. We walked a bit further and sat under a tree where he showed us what he had, and he had plenty. We were just about out of water, and he offered us some, but it was at his home, which was a good hike from where we were. He was on a small horse and there were plenty of Brahma bulls and cows from whence came the hongos. We walked to a huge Ceiba tree in the middle of nowhere. We asked him if we could pose for some pictures on his small horse. I felt bad for the horse when Randy decided to get on since he too was a big guy and heavier than Jerry. Jerry didn't get on the horse. We marched on the tree was about halfway where he lived. It was far, but we finally made it to the farmer's house. He invited us in and had a plastic drum with not much water in it, but happily shared it, pouring it into the canteen. He gave us about a half-gallon, since he didn't have too much. In his house we saw that he had mushrooms everywhere drying out. We bought about three-quarters of a pound for about sixty dollars. We were happy and decided to head on back. It was a long, long walk back to Mayabell. We must have gone through about five different gates, which we shut each time we went through one. We didn't know if we were trespassing or who's land we were on. The farmer assured us that it was okay. There was a small creek that we had to cross on a make-shift bridge made of an old four by four piece of wood going across the creek with a guide wire to hold onto. We made it to the end of the dirt road and on to the paved one leading back to Mayabell.

It was time to prepare some food, more soup. We invited Chris to eat with us and he brought some bananas to share. He was telling us that we had to go to Agua Azul. It was a series of waterfalls with turquoise blue water in the middle of the jungle. It sounded wonderful, but that would be on our list of must sees next time. We smogged out later that evening as we were so tired from our marathon walk. The travelers we met there at Mayabell were very cool people, many were European hippies. We always share a smoke with our "kind." We know that it could be us looking for some. We crashed hard, but not before we had a few spores to end the day.

Day 8

Last day. We went for another walk to the ruins and took it all in once again. We decided to go out the main entrance and walked down the road a short way and saw another path leading to more sets of waterfalls. It was a muddy path. When we got to the waterfalls it was beautiful. There were some big rocks we climbed to the top. The rocks weren't even slippery at all and we made it to the top. It was secluded and had a primeval look. This is the way it has been for probably hundreds, if not, thousands of years. We spent a couple of hours there, it was nice. We headed back to Mayabell to prepare for our return to Texas. I gave the rest of our camping fuel and ice chest to the guy working there whom we paid. At Mayabell, the travelers were allowed to store their backpacks in a room in the home where he lived while they were out at the ruins. We had to lighten our load before we headed out. We had eaten most of our canned food so that made it much lighter.

5. Return to Texas, Mexico City

Day 9

We took a colectivo back to the town of Palenque. We were all dreading to get back on the train, and we certainly weren't going walk back the eight kilometers to the train station out of town. Well, we did. We didn't have too much money left among all of us, well, Jerry and I. We made it to the station and were tired as hell. There was a small open air waiting area with concrete benches to sit on. I took off my trail pad and laid it down on the bench and it felt surprisingly quite comfortable. We had to wait a few hours for the next train. In the meantime, we met this guy who was a psychologist from New York City traveling alone. We told him our story and all that had happened to us. I guess he felt sorry for us and gave us $50.00 U.S. Wow! That was so nice of him. It was surely going to help our situation big-time. The train arrived and we all rode to Mexico City. No one wanted to take the train back to Nuevo Laredo. That would take too long. So, upon arriving in D.F., we wandered out to find a telephone. We saw a Holiday Inn; it was a sight for sore eyes. We went in and Randy made a call to Clark, our friend back at home. Randy asked him if he could please wire $100 via Western Union to Laredo near the Hamilton Hotel, where he could pick it up. He did ask how the camera was doing and Randy said, "Great."

I decided to go and look for a bank to get a cash advance on my credit card. Jerry and I would go on the search, while Randy would remain with all of our gear at the Holiday Inn, and he was fine with that. So, Jerry and I start walking down the streets of downtown Mexico City. We had to pay careful attention because all of the street corners looked the same. While walking down a street I smelled something very familiar, pan dulce. I told Jerry that there was a bakery somewhere nearby and that we had to find it, which we did. We bought some and it was so good. We then saw a street vendor selling creamy ice cream on a stick which was also quite good. We did find a bank and I was able to get a small cash advance. We got back to the Holiday Inn and were ready to move on. We got directions to the Central del Norte bus station and began our hike. I bought a small iron on patch of a colorful mushroom, it said Soy Feliz (I'm Happy). We were walking down the Paseo de la Reforma Avenue and we had to rest. There was a grassy area underneath "El Angel de la Independencia" monument. We rested there for a while. We continued and were just outside of the bus station. We still had some weed with us but didn't want to take a chance bringing any across into Texas. Taking it into Mexico, no problem, but from Mexico into Texas, problem. I don't think so. Quickly, we had to find a safe place to burn. On the highway by the bus station there was a grassy median with trees and traffic speeding on both sides. We just sat there smoking about four or five joints. When we finished, we crossed over to the bus station. We needed three one-way tickets to Nuevo Laredo, but we only had enough money for two. I asked the ticket person if we could barter some of our stuff for a ticket. He asked what we had. Jerry's old camera, some portable binoculars, a survival knife, and a couple of flashlights. He said, "Let me go and ask the driver if he'll do it." He came back and said that it would be okay. Oh my God we were ecstatic. We got on the bus that evening and traveled through the night back to the border.

Day 10

We made it! Arriving in Nuevo Laredo we were in familiar territory finally. We still had to get across and we had all these mushrooms on us. We came across some public bathrooms where we stuffed the mushrooms in our crotches and boots. We looked beat. When we got to Customs we walked through and the agent said, "You guys look like you've been put through the ringer." We had, and he didn't even check our bags! How lucky was that? We made our way across the International Bridge. Back in the U.S.A.! We walked and found the Western Union office where Clark had wired Randy the $100. We made it to the parking garage at the Hamilton, but we had no key for the Jeep. We had to call a locksmith to make us a key. Good thing Clark had sent some cash. When we got the key, the Jeep would not start. The battery was dead. No problem, we'll just jump start it by popping the clutch. So, Randy and Jerry pushed the Jeep inside the garage. It would not start. I've done this many times before. Oh, I forgot to turn the key in the ignition. After that, on the first try it started. YEAH!!!!!!!!!!!!!!!! We were back on the road to San Marcos. It was quiet most of the way back. We all couldn't believe what we had just experienced. When we got back, I called my girlfriend at the time. It was nice to hear her voice. In the following days we would tell our friends of our adventure. They all wanted to go with us next spring break. Now that we blazed a trail, we knew a better way to do it. We still had plenty of time to plan before the next trip.

I've been wanting to put this in print for years. I used to tell my Spanish 3 classes this story when I was teaching a unit on Latin American Civilization. It always took the whole class period. I sometimes would have them take notes and then give a little quiz allowing them to use their notes. It was fun and I think they enjoyed listening. I think they appreciated a teacher who actually had some credibility on traveling through Mexico. I never told them about the weed and mushrooms, though. I love Mexico!

Message to Randy: Bro, it was water! It was water on the toilet seat at your parent's house! It was difficult to put that much to stay on the seat! You were so pissed off that I could not, for some reason, tell you the truth. Sorry. :)

22

6. TRIP TWO: MORE TRAILBLAZING WITH THE TAG-ALONGS

One year had passed and it was time for another spring break vacation. This time joining Jerry and me were Jerry's roommates, Clay, Rafael, and Dale. They wanted to tag along with someone who already knew the "ropes," so to speak. We made it unbelievably hard on ourselves on the first trip. We would do it smarter this time around. First, we would not take those big mother-fucking backpacks like we did before. Next, we would take the bus the whole way, traveling by night. I did some research navigating through Mexico City mainly with a Frommer's Mexico guidebook. We left on the Wednesday before we actually got out that Friday to get a head start. We took off for Laredo once again, this time in my Buick Regal. We parked in a covered lot outside of the Hamilton Hotel, not inside the parking garage like the previous year. We all pitched in for a taxi to take us across the border to the bus station in Nuevo Laredo. I took my brother's small boy scout backpack with a fold over flap and tie down. It was much lighter than the one I had taken last year, but it was still a little heavy. We did not bring any canned food this time. We would purchase all our food as we traveled. However, we each took one ounce of weed and were set. Everyone was "stoked" as Dale would say. He was also one of my former Spanish students at the university. He had long blond hair, typical surfer dude. He had a bumper sticker on his car that said "Surf Naked." Rafael spoke some Spanish with a Castilian accent, pronouncing the "s's and z's" with a "th" sound. Like talking with a lisp. I'm not sure of Clay's Spanish aptitude but was a very nice guy. Everyone got along very well. Remember Randy? Well, he was not interested at all in going. I didn't even ask him. We were still very good friends and made plenty of trips together to Cozumel. He was a scuba instructor, which is how we had met back in '83. Those stories will come later in the book.

We boarded the bus in Nuevo Laredo and headed to Mexico City. Once there we would take the subway from the Central del Norte station to the TAPO station (Terminales de Autobuses Ponientes Orientes). It was getting dark when we boarded about 7 P.M. This time it would take fifteen hours rather than twenty-five to get to the D.F. I told the guys not to spark up in the bus while we were traveling. Jerry and I were seated in the front of the bus and the other three were seated in the back by the restroom. After about an hour or so we passed the Federales checkpoint. As we traveled a bit more, suddenly Jerry and I noticed that someone sparked up a doobie! *Shit!* I thought. *What the hell are they thinking?* I walked to the back and told them to put it out. Though it didn't seem to bother anyone on the bus. Even the bus driver didn't say anything. Traveling through the night we made a couple of stops in the middle of nowhere. It was cold, windy, and everyone had to get off the bus. We would buy a snack or coffee or something. After traveling in the morning, we arrive in Mexico City and walk a little way down to get on the Metro, the subway. It's very cheap, like ten cents, and we get off at the TAPO terminal. It was dome-shaped with a green roof and huge! It looked like a small "Astrodome." There were all these different company bus lines with ticket windows all around. We purchased our tickets to Villahermosa, as there were no direct routes available to Palenque. It was a waiting game. We waited for a few hours, sitting around. Normally I am impatient but traveling I have learned to be more patient. I sometimes get lost in my thoughts, but hopefully I always have something to read. Eventually we board for Villahermosa and are off on our next "leg" of the trip.

7. BUSING THROUGH TO LA RUTA MAYA, MAYABELL

We make it to Villahermosa in the early evening, but there were not any buses leaving for Palenque until the following morning. We had just missed the last bus. We hung around the bus station and walked around taking turns going for a smoke and watching the backpacks. We found some street vendors and had some tacos. Dang, it was turning out to be a lot smoother than the last trip. No trains! Most Mexicans travel through Mexico by bus. They have their shit together about that and it's not expensive at all. Villahermosa is in the state of Tabasco. It's lush, but not quite jungle like Chiapas.

It's morning and we catch our bus to Palenque. It takes around two hours or so. At least the bus station in Palenque is in town. I recommended that they get a blanket while we were here. We also bought honey to transport the mushrooms while traveling, along with getting some snacks. Before we leave for the archaeological zone, we headed to a restaurant for a good breakfast so that we can have plenty of energy. We make it to Mayabell. The campground is nice. There are palapas around the perimeter also some in the interior. It's first come, first served. Since there were five of us traveling, I was hoping that we would be able to get a palapa. Most of the palapas can hold three or four hammocks. Well, it seemed that they were taken, except one. There was one, but there were only a pair of sandals on the corner. No backpacks or gear or anything. The guys said, "Oh well, we'll take this one." A short time later a couple of guys show up. They didn't tell us anything. I felt bad about it, but oh well. Those guys had taken up next to our palapa. We had some mushrooms later that night and it really messed up my trip. I kept getting these negative vibes. Since my hammock was on the edge of the palapa I was closest to them. I had to have my back turned towards them and couldn't look at them.

The next morning, we would head to the ruins going in through the back entrance once again. We showed the guys the mushroom road. We checked out the ruins, the guys were blown away just as Jerry and I were also once again. We spend some time there at the ruins checking everything out. We went down into the tomb of Pacal. We're tired and head on back to Mayabell and have supper at the restaurant. They serve good and inexpensive food. Their menu also has a good selection of dishes.

What we really wanted was to go and pick our own mushrooms, but we had to get up very early and had to be in the fields picking by 3 A.M. This meant that we had to leave no later than 1:30 A.M.

We're up early and head out by 1:35 A.M., and it's a very long walk to the mushroom fields. We cross the creek and walk a few miles past to get to the fields. Soon we're there. We spread out to look for the cow patties from which they grow. We see the campesinos picking mushrooms as well. They were probably thinking, *damn these gringos, infringing on their turf.* They didn't seem to be bothered by our presence, picking alongside them. We smiled and said "buenos días." We tried picking away from where they were, giving them their space. We all had brought some bags to put the shrooms in. It was dark and cool with the calf high grass all wet with dew. We picked until just after the sun came up but were far away from the make-shift bridge over the creek. We walk alongside the creek looking for a narrow place to jump across. We decided to rest a little under a tree by the creek where we would jump over to the other side. We jumped and I barely made it across. My foot got a little wet, it hit the edge of the water. We headed back to Mayabell with a feeling of accomplishment. I wanted to have an experience unlike any other and decided that I would consume a large quantity of mushrooms, more than I have ever had. But first I wanted to go up into the jungle to get some firewood so that we could have a fire. Now, our palapa was on the back row of the campground second from the left as you're walking towards the back of the Mayabell campground. There was a tree line on the other side of the barbed-wired fence of dense unspoiled jungle. We all started up the hill gathering wood while making small piles by the trail while making our way up. We had to be careful because of the ants. Often when picking up a piece of wood it would have ants on it. I remember climbing up and looking around. Thinking, *Shit, easy to get turned around and get lost, since everywhere around looked alike*. It was steamy and hot. We were all sweaty and decided we had plenty of firewood for the night. I remember the next day, Clay had taken a walk into the forest to take a leak. After a while I said, "Where's Clay?" He still hadn't returned. We yelled for him, and he walked out about twenty yards from where he had entered. He had gotten turned around. It was our yelling for him that gave him his bearings. Whew! We had a light supper before our main event. The effect of mushrooms is greater on an empty stomach. After that long hike I needed to get a little something in my belly.

8. SPACE TRUCKIN'

As dusk was approaching, I only had one thing in mind, tripping like never before. Eating mushrooms before, I had only had two or three caps or a couple of "little bad boys" as Jerry used to say. They were small, a cap and stem. The mushrooms are off-white and have some brown on top and underneath the cap is dark. If you pinch the end of the stem, it turns a bluish purple. If it is white underneath, then you know that they aren't the right ones. While there was still light, I went back to the palapa and sat on my hammock with a baggie full of the spores. I started eating. I had some fresh ones with a little honey along with some dried ones. Some don't like the taste, but it doesn't bother me. I ended up eating about an ounce or more, never having eaten that much before.

It usually takes around thirty minutes or so for the mushrooms to kick in. For me it starts with the "yawns." I start yawning and yawning and I know it's only a short time after that. Sometimes afterwards it messes with my stomach and must go and sit on the pot. It's usually then when the floor and the walls start "breathing." Then if I move my finger or hand in the air I can see "tracers" following. Well, I did have to go to the bathroom. I would rather go early in the "trip" than later. So, I went quickly and as I started back it started kicking in. I tried to stay on the path back to our palapa seeking out my hammock and weed to roll one. As I lay in my hammock, I'm facing toward the entrance of the campground and could see a couple of cars' headlights. I just knew it was the police and they were there to get us. I started trying to not think about that. I just started hearing a lot of sounds. The other guys were tripping as well, but not like me, I'm pretty sure. Suddenly, I'm hearing everything in our palapa, then I start hearing all these conversations at the same time. It was all the conversations happening in the campground at the same time. I could distinctly understand every one of them simultaneously. I couldn't believe it. Then it happened, I see these colorful ribbons of light across the campground. Then it's like I'm within the streaks of light. The ribbons of light were moving from our palapa to the entrance of Mayabell. I raced around, by raced, I mean flying or soaring. All the while still laying in my hammock! My consciousness was no longer in my physical body, and I left the campground toward the road and then headed up towards the sky. I just kept going until I could see the Earth below. *What in the ...?* I thought. I figured I would go further and went past the moon, then past Mars it was orangy colored. There was what seemed like a small gap between the next giant planets. I flew by Jupiter and Saturn. I was looking at the freaking rings! I was getting closer to the edge of the solar system then there was darkness. I started to get a little scared and decided to go back cause shit man, I didn't want to get "lost." Somehow, I raced back to Earth and back into my palapa. *What the fuck had just happened?* I'm not sure how much time had elapsed. I told my friends that I had just taken a trip!

After smoking some weed, we all had decided to take a walk. We walked down the road toward the ruins. It was night, but I could see like if it was daytime. We walked around the corner heading to the main entrance of the ruins. On the curve to the right is the trail leading to a series of waterfalls. It's dark as fuck and we're walking down a jungle trail with one small penlight one of the guys had. As we were getting closer you could hear the falls getting louder and louder. We hung around for not too long before we made our way back to Mayabell. What a night. I've never eaten that many magic mushrooms again. I have found in my personal experiences that many of the people who I know who have taken psychedelics are usually better-balanced people. A bit more calm, thoughtful, and laid back. My friends and I take more of a personal growth purpose, rather than to just take them for fun's sake. They are fun. When young King Pacal came into power in Palenque, and he was "expected" to consume the mushrooms in order to gain insight to better lead his people. I read an article a couple of days ago on Apple News, it said that MDMA, magic mushrooms, LSD, and Ketamine are having a renaissance being researched and used it psychotherapy. It allows people connecting to themselves and others without the anxiety that it normally brings them. It was very interesting, and I can see some people reaping the benefits. On the TV news I heard a report where they are using psilocybe muchrooms in the treatment of PTSD in veterans with positive results. I'm not saying that mushrooms are for everyone, and I haven't had any for over thirty years. It would be interesting to eat a couple of caps just to get that primeval feeling again. However, my wife, Ladema, is not one who would partake of mushrooms, no matter what. Not interested which is fine by me.

9. AGUA AZUL, PLAYA ZIPOLITE, OUR LADY OF GUADALUPE

We decided that it was time to move on. Jerry and I wanted to go to Agua Azul and San Cristóbal as suggested by our Swiss friend, Chris Ubmann, from the previous year. We take a "colectivo" back to the town of Palenque looking for a bus to Agua Azul. Only the second class bus station has buses going in the direction of Agua Azul and San Cristóbal. We get into what amounts to a beat-up old-school bus. Looks don't matter to us at all, as long as it gets us to where we need to go. We'll get off at the "crucero." It's a crossroads. To the right or north is Agua Azul and continuing down the road ahead or west down a few hours is San Cristóbal, a cool picturesque little town in the mountains. Well, the road down to Agua Azul is very curvy. It winds down and down. In order to cut some time off, we decided to take shortcuts using a muddy trail where we went slip sliding away. We were all muddy, but we did shave off some time. We had about an hour of sunlight left and had to find some lodging. We walked a little way and asked around. There was an indigenous woman who would allow travelers to hang their hammocks in an empty shell of a white house. We walked to the house and saw that there were already quite a few people inside who had their hammocks strung up. There was no more room inside, but there was no one on the covered porch where we decided "home" would be for the night. We strung up our hammocks across the porch. We all fit snuggly with a clear view of the falls. It was a little damp from the spray of the falls. It was cool. There was a little restaurant there on site where we got some snacks and beer. That was it. The white house and jungle. The next day we got up early and walked further down the trail up the river. I recognized the trail when the movie "Predator" came out with Arnold. It was filmed there. The water I heard has particles of turquoise which gives it the bluish color. When it rains it doesn't look blue. We swam some and got ready to head back up to the "crucero" to catch a ride to San Cristóbal de las Casas. We head on our way and it's a long walk back up. We all decide to pose for a group picture alongside the road which I blew up to a 20 by 30 poster. I still have it. Well, we make it to the top of the road and wait for the next bus to stop, heading to San Cristóbal. While we're waiting for the bus, I'm chatting with the guy there in the booth just off of the road. I hear a woman speaking, and it wasn't Spanish, so I ask, "What language is she speaking?" He said, "Tzeltal." A Mayan dialect. Oh, okay, cool. We get on the bus after waiting about an hour. It's a second- or third-class bus, like a beaten old school bus. We all started to hang our clothes out the window to try and dry them. It's hard to get your clothes to dry with so much humidity. We had a pit stop in the little town of Ocosingo. It was immaculately clean. The streets were swept very nicely. Good cup of coffee.

We get to San Cristóbal, and it is a very nice stop. We spent the rest of the day there. I ask around looking for the market. I asked someone where the market was, and they pointed to a building. We go in and walk downstairs, a little confused. Fuck! It was the meat market. Oh my, the smell was horrendous. I held my breath as long as I could as I made my way out.

Eventually, we found the crafts market outside of the Santo Domingo church. People were selling all kinds of cool stuff like clothing from Guatemala. They had some cool pants. We didn't spend the night as we were heading to the Pacific Coast. So, we bought a ticket to Oaxaca and slept during the night. The following morning on our way to Oaxaca we stopped somewhere by a roadside café on a mountain. We bought some coffee and proceeded to sip it on the edge of a cliff on the mountain that we were on. It was beautiful. We were all looking down this wooded canyon. You could see the smoke

32

rising from the home fires. It looked surreal. The coffee tasted great. On the way as the bus was winding down the road, I looked out the window and could see that the bus was right on the edge of the road! I had to turn away as it was too fucking scary. We get to Oaxaca later in the morning. It was cold as we are up in the mountains. We spend the day walking around town and the main square by the church. We took some photos. While in a shop near the market we even ran into some friends Jerry and the guys knew from San Marcos. I was buying a colorful orange Mexican blanket with thick green stripes. Small world, no? As they say. Jerry's girlfriend, Kim, was with her friends in Acapulco. We entertained the idea of going there, but we had heard about the Federales checkpoints on the way and we had mushrooms and weed. We couldn't get a ticket to Puerto Angel but had to get one to Pochutla. It was maybe ten minutes to Puerto Angel. We had heard they had nice beaches. From Pochutla, we took a taxi to Puerto Angel. I asked the driver, "Which is the nicest beach?" He says, "El Zipolite." As we're getting close, he says "Cuidado con los Marineros," "Watch out for the Marineros." They were Federales, the beach version and dressed in black uniforms where you can't see them at night. We all thanked him for the warning. He drove us to a small house on the beach where this lady had a little palapa attached to her house with a view of the beach. It cost us only $3.00 U.S. to hang our hammock and all meals! We were all ready to chill the fuck out. The beach it turns out is swimsuit optional. Dale, the surfer guy, is bound and determined to surf naked, just like his bumper sticker says. The waves would break short and hard near the shore and would throw you onto the sand. It was a mean riptide, and I did not want to get in it. I got in as shallow as I could. It was fun watching him surf. Quite a few surfers there. He just borrowed a surfboard and was a happy camper. Life is good. We ate and it was getting dark. It had been a few days since I've had any mushrooms, so I decided to have a few. We made a little campfire on the beach and sat in a circle chatting with some locals. One of the locals had a t-shirt with a red cross and "Papel Higiénico" on the front of it. "Toilet Paper," it said. That soon became my favorite word for a long time after that moment. We're sitting there passing a joint and smoking cigarettes. The joint was passed to me, and I gave it to Jerry.

Out of the blackness of night we all heard, "Levanten las manos!" What the F…? We were surrounded by the Marineros. They were all dressed in black and proceeded to lock and load their assault rifles pointed at us. They smelled the weed. I stand up followed by the rest of the guys except Dale. I'm thinking, *We're fucked.* Dale who was still sitting on the beach and passed out face first. One of the Marineros started looking for the "roach" that Jerry had put in the sand. They thought it was a "roach." But in fact, it was a cigarette butt. Thank goodness for Jerry's quick thinking. He had eaten the roach. The Marinero found the cigarette butt and I immediately pointed out that it indeed was only a cigarette butt. Remember we were all tripping, and this had abruptly made us stone cold sober. I was starting to feel queasy and asked the head Marinero if I could walk a few feet away to throw up. So, I walk away a few feet and bent over, but nothing. I came back to the group. The head guy was asking where the marijuana was. We really didn't have any. I told him that we were trying to score some. I surely didn't want them going through our stuff since we had mushrooms. I thought, *maybe if I come clean with them.* I told the head guy, "Yes we were indeed smoking weed, but it was our last joint," and that we were looking for some. With that he said, "Vamonos" We were going to be taken to jail. I knew that would be a mistake if we left the beach. So, I asked the head guy, "Señor Honorable, le puedo dar una moneda?" "Honorable Sir, may I give you some coin?" He answered "¿Cómo cuánto? "Like how much?" Now at the time Mexico had devalued their peso and it was $500 pesos to $1 U.S. or something like that. I knew that we didn't have much money, so I told him, "Mil quinientos." "Fifteen hundred." They all broke out laughing their asses off. I had only offered them $3.00 U.S. I told them that I was a college professor and that we had to get back to the border in a couple days and didn't have enough. Finally, he accepted my offer, we all had to pay them $3.00 each. A fifteen-dollar bribe for five guys is unheard of. I know that there had to be some divine intervention. There just had to be. This was miracle number one. They took the cash and disappeared into the darkness. I could still hear them chuckle as they walked away. What the fuck had just happened? At that moment, Dale picks his head up with his face covered in sand. It was so funny. He said, "I can't believe I lost it, I can't believe I lost it." Right then Clay, Rafael, and Dale proceeded to our palapa and went straight to bed. They were all shook up pretty good. Jerry and I on the other hand, were still wired. We walked over to a big round palapa looking for some weed to smoke. Had to take the edge off. We walked in and were welcomed. We introduced ourselves. Someone asked, "Hey was it you guys that got busted?" "Yeah, it was us." We asked is it cool to smoke here, with the Marineros around. "Yeah," they said. They don't come to the palapas. They stay on the beach. We were still on the beach, but further back. We talked for a couple of hours, sharing stories. One of the locals was telling that the police chief's daughter had a boyfriend that he didn't like and had his men pick him up. They put a towel in his mouth and got two bottles of carbonated water with crushed chili peppers in and brought the bottles to his nose so that he had inhale the chili infused water. I told him to stop as it was making me sick to my stomach. We soon made our way to our palapa and respective hammocks. It had been a long day. The other guys were sound asleep, sleeping like babies. Hehe!

The following morning the nice lady made us some breakfast. I told her that we would be leaving later that afternoon and if she had a shower we could use. She said no, but that a woman up the road did. I needed a bath something terrible. Me and the guys take turns, and I went and knocked on the door. The woman answered and said it would be 25 cents. I took my canteen to fill it up, might as well. I filled the canteen and looked at it and saw all kinds of black particles floating in it. I dumped and rinsed it with clean water later. Back at our palapa the guys are still kind of in a daze. We pass some time when some "artesanos," artisans stop by to show us their wares. It was two guys, very nice with cool artwork. We talked until we get ready to leave for Pochutla to catch a bus to Oaxaca, Mexico City, then to Nuevo Laredo. After the artisans leave, we're getting our gear together, when Jerry and Dale both yell, "Hey man, I can't find my wallet." Both guys look and look. The woman's son came by with a rake to help us look in the sand. I kept running through my head, that I didn't see anything suspicious. We're all extremely vigilant. The son said that he thought the artesanos had ripped us off. They were such nice guys. The mood goes down AF. Bummed out, we catch our taxi, to catch the bus. I'm thinking, *we're f'd, low on money to get back.* We'll just have to conserve, everyone pitching in to get us back. It was a long road back. We pulled into Pochutla and got tickets to Oaxaca. We at least had enough to get us there. We were all tired and hungry and did not want to spend any of what little money we had on food. Everyone is on the sidewalk just standing around, waiting. Rafael said, "I'll be back," and started walking down a way. I decided to take a load off and proceeded to sit on the street curb. It was on the main drag in Pochutla. I started praying to God, asking to help us get back home. I have my head down on my crossed arms which are on my knees. Then, I prayed to La Virgén de Guadalupe, asking for the same. I was born on December 12, which is the day she appeared to Juan Diego. She is my patron saint, along with the whole of Mexico. As I looked down between my knees to the street, I see a pile of cash between my feet! What the …? It was all pesos, different denominations and colorful. I instantaneously look around and there is no one nearby. But, as I looked up, I see across the street that there was a shrine to the Virgin! At that moment, both Jerry and Dale say, "Hey man, I found my wallet," and the other said, "me too." Then, Rafael comes back with food, eating a taco and smiling. Both Jerry and Dale say that their wallets were right there inside on top. A kind woman at a restaurant had given Rafael some food out of generosity. He told her about our circumstances. I then grabbed a handful of cash and gave to Rafael to go back and pay the nice lady for the food she had given him. Also, to get some more food and give her a generous tip. Jerry looked at me with a "what in hell just happened" look. I just shrugged my shoulders with a I don't know response. With the rest of the cash, I walked across the street and stuffed the rest of the money in through a slot in the donation box by the Virgin's shrine. I didn't keep any of the money, which was a lot. I did not count it, but there was quite a bit. We couldn't believe what had just happened. I don't tell that story, kind of unbelievable. It's even hard for me to believe! But I know it really happened. And no, we weren't tripping or anything like that. Who wants people to think that they are crazy? I did tell my mother thirty years later during one Christmas in 2017. I didn't even ask her if she believed me. But, just so you know, I did tell two of my rehabilitation teachers at CCRC in Austin, and one of them just told me that she didn't believe me. To the other teacher, I sent a rough draft of this chapter to get her opinion, which was kind of important to me. She has not yet responded. I sent it in 2019! We have not corresponded since. I still respect her very much: she is a very cool lady. I guess I spooked her.

It's time to board the bus for Oaxaca. We would get there around five in the morning. We never talked about what had happened there in Pochutla.

10. BACK TO TEXAS

We arrived in Oaxaca very early in the morning at the bus station, it is cold AF. We all use our blankets to cover up as we're walking through the station. Well, all except Dale. He didn't get a blanket and only used the poncho he brought with him. He was feeling sick and didn't look too good. Walking through the station we saw a couple of men laying on the benches covered with newspapers. Rafael saw this and covered one of them with his own blanket. The other guy started laughing and told him, "You know he's going to sell it for some booze." It didn't matter, the sun would come up soon and begin to warm us up. We caught a bus as soon as we could for Mexico City. We all were ready to get back home, and we were still far away. It's still better than being in a jail cell! We travel to D.F. and get there late in the evening at the TAPO station. We were going to have to take the subway back to the Central del Norte station. We decided we would take a taxi instead. It was dark and late, and we wanted to get there as soon as possible. We barter with the taxi driver, trading the usual, flashlights, a little money, small pair of binoculars, and a couple of knives. We were able to catch the last bus heading to Nuevo Laredo. We travel through the night and arrive around mid-morning. Again, we pitch in to take a taxi across the border and get dropped off at the Hamilton covered parking lot. Ah, we made it! I go to start the car and it won't start. The transmission light is on. I check the fluid level and there is none. I usually do not carry transmission fluid in my car, but I do carry a quart of oil just in case. Well, someone said "You can use the oil, it'll work." I saw no other option as it was sort of an emergency, so I put some in. The car started right up, and we made it back to San Marcos surprisingly with no problems. I drove around with the oil in the transmission for months afterward, probably half a year until I had to have the transmission replaced. Well, that was trip number two. I think everyone was satisfied.

11. TRIP THREE: THIRD YEAR IN A ROW, HIGHLIGHTS

The following summer of '88 I met a girl who was a former university student of mine. She eventually became my girlfriend and ex-wife. She was an adventurous girl who wanted a travel adventure. I told her of my trips to Chiapas and Cozumel. She seemed excited and ready to go on a trip. We went the following November during the Thanksgiving holidays. It was the usual bus trip, Nuevo Laredo, Mexico City, Villahermosa, Palenque. We traveled through Mexico City without any problems. We were just out of Mexico City, near Puebla, when the torta that Laura had at the TAPO bus station with that special sauce and stuff, was not settling well in her stomach. She asked the bus driver if she could get the key to the bathroom. He said, "No funciona." Shit! Out of order. I then grabbed a couple of plastic bags from my backpack so that she could use to throw up in. I like taking some plastic bags or zip-loc baggies for emergencies like this one. Thanks to my quick thinking, it was just in time. She got a little bit on her t-shirt and ended up throwing it in the trash at the Puebla bus station.

We made it to Palenque without any more problems. That first afternoon at Mayabell, I was just chilling in my hammock when five or six girls from Italy or France, I'm not sure, were in front of the laundry tables with water faucets. Well, they all started taking off their clothes right freaking there! They proceeded to climb into the wash basins and bathe in the place where you do laundry. These are what I like to call God's little gifts to mankind. Mayabell does have men's and women's private showers. I guess it's just a European thing.

At the ruins, there was a mound to the right of the Temple of Inscriptions, and it had started to be excavated from the bottom. On my very last trip, some years later, the complete temple would be revealed, and I would enter it. While in the restaurant there at the ruins, we were befriended by young Lacandón family. The guy's name was Bol, and I can't remember what his wife's name was. She was one of the many granddaughters of one of the chiefs of the village of Najá, Chan Kin Viejo. I asked Bol if he was still alive, and he said "Chan Kin vive." Next thing their little girl is eating all of my scrambled eggs, but it doesn't matter she was so cute. A couple of months later in *National Geographic* magazine there's a picture of Bol at the Palenque ruins. I believe it came out in the January issue. You can check it out for yourselves. At Mayabell we met a journalist from El Salvador. A real nice guy who drove the whole way, just to get to some Palenque mushrooms. I no longer went in search of the spores. I did not want to take anymore unnecessary risks. A couple of days later, we see him smiling really big with bits and pieces of mushrooms in his teeth. It was funny. He only had one cassette to listen to on his trip. I really regret not giving him any of mine and I had plenty. He even gave Laura a couple of cool crystals. In hindsight, I should have given him all my cassettes.

We were going to go to San Cristóbal, but I did not want to make the five-to-six-hour bus ride. So, while we were in the town of Palenque, I noticed a sign in a travel agency door that there indeed were flights out of Palenque. We decided to check it out. I didn't even know Palenque had an airport. We purchased a one-way ticket to Tuxtla Gutierrez for $23 U.S. We would have to catch a bus in Tuxtla to San Cristóbal and it was only an hour away. The travel agency lady drove us to the airport. There was a tiny building and a small landing strip. There were fields around with tall grass. We waited a short while, then another woman who was making the trip with us said, "Mira, allí viene," and she points to the sky. A small prop plane comes into view. It lands, we board quickly, and we're off. We fly over the Palenque ruins while I'm listening to music with my headphones and taking pictures. Just taking it all in. It was pretty cool seeing the landscapes of Chiapas. Well, we took a taxi from the Tuxtla airport, which was very nice and modern, to the Tuxtla bus station. We must wait around an hour to catch the next bus to San Cristóbal. We catch the bus and travel through Chiapa de Corzo. I remember seeing the famous monument there as we drove by through town. We make it to San Cristóbal. There the air is fresh, and my new girlfriend is quite impressed. We get a room at the Capri hotel on the main drag a few blocks from the town square. After being there a couple of days and eating, I start to get sick. I'm throwing up, feeling feverish with chills, no bueno. I only had three joints left to make it back. I decided to eat some burned toast to help me get rid of the stomach bug. Since that trip, I always carry activated charcoal capsules in my first-aid kit. We ended up getting a direct ticket to Mexico City then to Nuevo Laredo. We make it back to San Marcos without any problems. Another fun trip!

12. TRIP FOUR: SPANISH CLUBBERS AND THE LONG ROAD BACK HOME

In December of 1990 I turned thirty on the twelfth, got married on the fourteen, and got my Master's on the twenty-first. My girlfriend, Laura, had become my wife and moved out to the cottage to live with me out in the country. I had been working in a small scenic central Texas school district in the hill country. I got hired in October of 1989 to teach Spanish. I started teaching Spanish I and II but added Spanish III and IV AP the following years. I had been wanting to take another trip down to Chiapas, possibly even taking a few students with me. I surely didn't want to take just anyone. I decided on inviting the Spanish Club Officers. My only requirement for them was to be passing all their classes. They were all passing except for the club president. She also happened to be the daughter of the School Board President! I would be taking two girls and a guy. The school board president drove us to the bus station in Nuevo Laredo. I would have my best friend, Jim, pick us up and drive us back to Central Texas. As soon as we walked into the bus station waiting room, I saw the culture shock on the girls' faces when they saw some people crawling on their knees to a shrine that was in the station. I told the girls that they were probably thanking a saint for a completed promise, or something like that. We board and it's the usual bus trip, I'm getting used to it already sort of. I did get three Valium pills to help me sleep on the bus. In Mexico City we decide to take the Metro and you know the doors close quite quickly. I had to grab Brent by the shirt to pull him in before he would have gotten left behind.

We get a nice suite with three bedrooms in the downtown area. We went out for dinner and turned in early to hit the road in the

42

morning. We make it to Mayabell and are able to get a big palapa. There's some extra space where some guys ask if they can hang their hammocks. Sure, no problem. My hammock would be the closest to theirs. They let me have some of their aguardiente, Mexican moonshine, and "toke" couple of hits.

Later that afternoon, we took the back way into the ruins. We walked the muddy trail before climbing these huge roots up the steep hill. We saw old women, probably grandmothers, doing the climb. When we made it to the top, I took a picture of all of us putting our muddy shoes towards the middle of a circle. I was the only one who decided to wear shorts. I knew that it would be hot, muddy, and wet. It had drizzled a bit as well. I'm not sure if they were ever able to get their clothes dried.

At the main plaza we climbed up and then went down into Pacal's tomb at the bottom of the Temple of Inscriptions. We also climbed the Tower at the Palace. The kids were very impressed. We took some great pics. It was nice. They couldn't believe that they were there. While up on the tower we decided it was time to leave, but there were so many Asian tourist climbing up the stairwell up to where we were. Now there isn't that much space up. As soon as I saw a Mexican, I yelled, "Párale allí amigo, déjanos bajar!" I told him to wait so that we could climb back down. We must have spent three or four days there at the ruins. then we decided to head to San Cristóbal for New Year's Eve. We didn't make it to Agua Azul this time. Perhaps next time. It seemed like a long road to San Cristóbal, that's because it was. We got some rooms at a small little hotel. The rooms were nice with fireplaces. I was wondering how it was going to get lit. There were a couple of pieces of firewood along with another piece that was very oily. I think that it was ocote pine and a very good fire-starter. Sure enough, it starts up quickly with only one match. We go out for dinner and a nightcap. I allowed the kids get one drink. They were all seniors and it was, after all, New Year's Eve. The next day we go shopping just outside the Santo Domingo Church and the girls get one of those colorful Guatemalan jackets that were popular at the time, and all kinds of cool stuff. Everyone is dreading getting on the bus. There are no routes available to Mexico City and decide to go back to Villahermosa, bypassing Palenque. About halfway we pull into a little roadside store, and I take a picture of the three girls. Laura was smiling and the other two were frowning. That set the mood and sort of threw me for a loop. I seemed to be intent on getting back asap. I thought of getting everyone a one-way flight, but that would have been way too expensive. So, when we finally got to the Villahermosa bus station rather than taking a bus, we decided it might be faster to take a taxi to Veracruz. It wasn't. The taxi driver will drive us for $100 U.S. each. That's a steep price and the taxi is a small compact car. It's getting late and decide to go for it. We get in and head for Veracruz. We all squeezed into cramped quarters for the night. It was sooo uncomfortable. Everyone was miserable. I saw one of the buses that had left the Villahermosa at the same time we had. It was also going to Veracruz. I just kept thinking what a mistake I had made by not taking a bus. Somewhere between Villahermosa and Veracruz in the middle of the night, the taxi driver said, "Hey you know that this town is the witch capital of Mexico." It was Acayucán. I told him to be careful going through here. We were on the highway and there was no one around, no cars on the road. Well, it was a long road to Veracruz. As we pulled into the bus station, I saw the bus that had left Villahermosa at the same time as us. It was a costly mistake taking the taxi. I went into the station and got tickets to Tampico. We were all so tired after the ride. At least now we'd be able to have our own seat on the bus and ride a bit more comfortably. We got to Tampico around mid-morning and would not be leaving until later that afternoon for Matamoros. I decided to get a room across the street so that we could shower and get a little rest before we would leave. It seemed to take forever, the waiting.

I would have liked to have been able to go to the ruins of El Tajín. They were nearby. There's a cool pyramid there.

We would arrive in Matamoros the following morning and I'd have to call my uncle Benny for a ride or something. We get to the border at Matamoros and take a taxi across the U.S. First stop, McDonald's. I remember everyone had put all of their bus ticket stubs on the table and it was completely covered. I called my uncle, and he came from Harlingen to pick us up. I then called up Jim who was going to pick us up in Laredo. I caught him just in time. He was about to leave for Houston. We weren't supposed to be back for a day or two. It worked out perfectly. My uncle Benny had to get his van to Alice to get worked on so I drove it and dropped it off at my grandparents' house. We rested a bit and ate. Jim came in his van to pick us up and drove us back to central Texas. On the way to drop the kids off one of the parents was waiting for us on the road. They switched cars and I remember Janie saying, "It's been real." Yeah, it was all real. All in all, it was a good trip. I ended up doing a slide show at a school board meeting. They all seemed impressed that we all made it back. Later in the spring I was voted Teacher of the Year in that district. I'm pretty sure it was because of the trip. I didn't believe the person from the Central office that was telling me. I accepted the honor, but then wished I hadn't since I had all these essays to write. It will be around three years before I go again.

13. Trip Five: Mexico City, The Happy Campers, Escaping NAFTA

I was itching to get back to Chiapas. My next trip would be with kids who I would hand pick to go. No more pouting allowed. I had three students in mind. They were all boys who had three years of Spanish so they would be very familiar with the places we would be going and seeing. Nathan was a very cool kid, long hair, and a One-Act Play Best in State actor. His dad was in the music business and Nathan gave me a master cassette copy of Stevie Ray Vaughn's Texas Flood. Nathan's best friend at that time was a kid named Evers. He was a good kid, too. He had a lot of brothers and sisters who had also been students of mine as well. I had one of his sisters in my class a couple of years prior. Don was another good kid. He was in Spanish Club and had gone to one of the PASF conventions and was hilarious. He could sing and dance and was very smart. I remember he did the YMCA dance at one of the mixers and was the star of the mixer. He was a life-of-the-party kind of guy. These were the three who would accompany me on my next adventure.

Don's parents had planned a barbeque for us the weekend before we were to leave. I met Nathan and Don's parents who were very cool people like their kids. To entrust me to care for their kids and provide them with some of the best education opportunities that they will have, I take it very seriously. I did have to get legal affidavits in case they needed medical attention. I had a special folder in my backpack with all the information. I had taken a VHS cassette of a copy of National Geographic's "The Mexicans: Through Our Own Eyes." To this day this had been my favorite Nat.Geo. shows of all time. I liked it because it showed many of the places we were going to see. I especially liked the part where they show the falls of Agua

Azul. It showed how blue the water really is. It's amazing seeing them in the middle of the jungle. On this next trip we would be flying into Mexico City. We would be flying out of San Antonio and would meet at the airport. They all came from their little hamlet in the Hill Country in someone's truck. We met them at the airport, but they had parked illegally somewhere outside of the airport. One of them decided to move the truck to a nearby neighborhood. They were cutting it close as it was almost time to leave. Finally, he got back, I think it was Nathan. We boarded late in the afternoon and would arrive in Mexico City in the evening. As we were getting closer to Mexico City, I looked out my plane window and saw lights cover the entire valley. There were lights as far as we could see. What a sight it was! We were going to stay at Isabel, La Católica hotel in downtown. We arrived with no problems at the DF airport. We took a taxi from the airport, but the taxi dropped us off a couple of blocks from the hotel. We walked around and were sort of lost, but we eventually found the hotel. The front doors were huge and very old. The reception area was open and spacious with a big mural on one of the walls. We got a couple of rooms, for the guys and me and my wife. We walked around back to our rooms. It was an old hotel with a lot of character. I'm sure if the walls could speak there'd be all kinds of stories. It sufficed with all the necessities, bed, and hot water. We would go out on the town tomorrow to the Museo Nacional de Antropología and Chapultepec Park. Before retiring I told the guys that we were going to get something to eat. We all walked a couple of blocks before I see a place. It had a "trompo" just outside of the place. It's a skewer with piles of meat on it on a turntable and a heater. As it rotates it cooks the outer portion of the meat and the waiter cuts little chunks off into a corn tortilla. Man, my mouth is watering as I'm writing this. Anyway, I ordered some tacos al pastor and a refresco de manzanita. The tacos are seasoned pork with onion, tomato, cilantro, and a serrano pepper. Hmm hmm. So, I walk over to the guys and I told each one to get a bite and they were a little hesitant, that is until the first bite. They looked at me in amazement, like they had won the lotto or something. Then I had them chase it with a swig from my apple soda. Nathan, said "Oh that is sooo good." They all agreed. They then ordered some for themselves. We were in México! We head on back to the hotel and turned in. It had been a long day. I was just excited to be back in Mexico.

The next morning, we head out early. We headed to the National Museum of Anthropology. We had breakfast at a little café just outside of the museum. I remember that I wanted some coffee, I needed some coffee. So, we all order, Nathan and I ordered coffee with our breakfast. Well, the waiter shows up with what looked like a thimble. I looked at him and we both told the waiter "más." I told him to bring us a big cup of coffee and he looked us like we were crazy. He just shrugs his shoulders and comes back a short while later with bigger cups and says to us "Seguros?" Ya'll sure?" Yes, thank you. It was expresso I later realized. No lack of energy all day. We were wired on coffee. Good thing with all the walking that we did. I was about to check off one of my life's goals off my list, visiting the museum. We went in and there were all these different galleries that were huge rooms of different indigenous groups of Mexico. I was in awe of everything I saw. I know the kids were in awe as well. There was an actual mammoth in a lower gallery, but there were two things that made my jaw drop. As I turned the corner and entered a new room I saw the actual sun stone, the Aztec calendar. It was hanging on a wall in all its glory. It was several tons and huge. I just stood there looking at it in a daze. I couldn't believe that I was standing there. After I had my fill, I kept on walking and saw a dark room that was lit with black lights and in the back of the room behind glass in a box was the jade mask of Pacal. I had only seen it in pictures. I wished that I had a digital camera back then. We went outside and decided to sit down on the benches to rest a bit. Outside were some trees and replicas of the temples of Bonampak. Like the ones at Bonampak, they had murals on the inside. The colors were very vivid, unlike the ones in Bonampak that have faded quite a bit, being in the jungle and all. There was also a replica of the temple to Chaac, the Mayan rain god. What a memorable experience. There was an etching of the sarcophagus lid to Pacal's tomb from Palenque. I've seen the actual sarcophagus lid down in the tomb of the Temple of Inscriptions. I still want to visit again, and I did try but they're closed on Mondays. We spent about five hours there at the museum.

We then set out for Chapultepec Park. We walked up the hill to see the former military academy now turned into a museum. There was a cool looking black carriage that had belonged to Maximiliano who had proclaimed himself Emperor of Mexico. He had been put there by Napoleon. There were portraits of the Child Heroes, los Niños Héroes. These were the cadets who when the U.S. marines invaded Mexico those were the last cadets to defend the academy, against the professional soldiers of the U.S. One of the cadets wrapped himself in the Mexican flag and jumped off a cliff to his death, rather than surrender to the U.S. The bravery of the cadets is admired the world over. Even today at roll call they still call out the cadets by name to honor them. We walked back down the hill and took some pictures of the monuments to the child heroes. The boys all knew the story of the cadets and felt it an honor just to be there. It was a special feeling. It was getting time to leave D.F. and head south for Chiapas. We were going to bus the remainder of the trip to Palenque and back.

We travel at night through Villahermosa to Palenque. We get to Palenque the next morning. In town we bought blankets and snacks. Everyone is excited to be there including myself. It's still a dusty little town. It hadn't changed much since my first trip back in '86. We take a colectivo to the archaeological zone, to Mayabell. I love that place. *I wonder if it's changed,* I thought to myself. I think they had a new Mayabell sign just outside of the campground. We walked in and started looking for an empty palapa. As we were walking around, we start smelling that old familiar "smell." Nathan and Evers perked up a little. We did find an empty palapa and started to unpack. The guys didn't have hammocks yet. There's a guy that goes by every so often to sell hammocks. He was supposed to stop by tomorrow I find out from a guy working there at the campground. They decided to wait until tomorrow to buy a hammock rather than rent one. I always bring my own. You can get a pretty cool deal on them. They are the thin-stringed Yucatan hammocks, very comfortable. It's still early afternoon and decide to go to the ruins. It was raining so we all don our cheapo rain ponchos and head out on foot. About halfway there, I ask if everyone has their money and Don said he had left his wallet there in his backpack. I said, "Really?" he said "Yeah." I told him to go back and get it and we would wait right here for him. So, he takes off running. We in the meantime are waiting by the side of the road. While waiting I'm looking at the jungle and notice a cool little concave orange mushroom. Don became a Spanish teacher and world traveler. He would send me emails from Patagonia in South America or from China. He married a girl from Scotland and lived there for a while. He teaches at a private school in Central Texas. Well, soon enough Don gets back. We're all wet, but happy just to be there. We head on to the ruins and take the trail that goes in the back way to the ruins. The ruins were still accessible going in the back way, we didn't have to pay to get in. This was my fifth trip and I've never paid to get into the Palenque ruins. The main entrance is up the road about half a mile around the corner that curves to the left. Just before the curve is the trail to go to the other waterfalls. Anyway, we walked around for a couple of hours in awe of the place. We would come back again the next day and spend some more time. Both Nathan and Evers walked around bare-footed. Everywhere we went, they went barefooted. There were some places that were very rocky and uneven. My feet are too sensitive to do that, as much as

I would like to. More power to them both. It was muddy but that didn't bother them at all. We spent a couple of hours there at the ruins. We head on back to Mayabell for the first night.

When we returned, we gathered up some wood for a fire. I had bought this fire-starter at REI that came in a tube, like toothpaste. It worked pretty well. We all set up our hammocks and got ready to call it a day. Don had laid down on the ground to read his book. He propped up himself on his elbow. I was laying in my hammock chillin' and I looked at Dan and all of a sudden, I see a huge tarantula crawling up his arm. I told him, "Don, don't move, there's a spider on your arm." I grabbed my cap and swatted the spider off his arm. Everyone was like "Oh shit!" I thought, *Yeah, that was close, ¿no?* I reminded them that we were in a jungle and Don promptly sat up. That first night they slept on the ground. Unnerving as it was that was nothing to these guys. Pretty soon the howler monkeys started howling. Everyone freaks out the first time they hear them. These guys were no different. The night was cold, and since I shared a hammock, I stayed warm. Don, on the other hand froze his ass off. He said he couldn't get warm at all with the blanket he had. I told him that he would be warm for the rest of the trip. The jungle does get cold at night, sometimes really cold. I took out an emergency blanket and gave it to him. He lined his hammock with it and slept on it that way. The following morning, he woke up sweating. He said that he would rather sweat than freeze. Nathan and Evers were fine. No complaints whatsoever. They were all such cool kids. We head on back to the ruins and near the back entrance everyone was able to take a swing on a big jungle vine like Tarzan. That was fun. Palenque is such a cool place to come and feel close to nature and the ancient structures. Later on when we came back to the ruins the next day we started walking down the path and trail left of the Temple of Inscriptions as you're facing it. We were leaving the main complex on a trail through the jungle. There were one or two ruins near the outskirts. The boys got ahead of Laura and me. We couldn't see or hear them. We kept walking and I started to worry a little and started yelling for them. We soon saw them, and they said, "Hey we found a temple in the jungle! Follow us!" We did a little way into the jungle. Sure enough, there was some sort of temple covered in foliage. There was a small opening and I asked, "Did you guys go in?" They answered, "Just a little way." I told them that they were very lucky not to have gotten bitten by a snake. *It's a freaking jungle!* I say to myself! It would not have been good if anything bad were to happen to them. We decided to go into town to book some transportation for an excursion to Agua Azul. I'm curious just how much it's changed. We made the reservations, picked up some snacks, and head on back to Mayabell.

The following morning, they pick us up early, around 7:00 and we head on to Agua Azul. It's a nice day so we'll be able to do some swimming. So far on every trip the pool at Mayabell, yes, they have one, has never worked, at least when I've been there. We stopped at the Misol Ha waterfalls on the way to Agua Azul. It was nice and cool early in the morning. The bus drops us off at the top of a hill and we must do a little hiking. We get a group pic with the falls in the background. The water looks very cold. We get back on the bus and continue further where we turn right at the crucero and head down the winding road till we get to the bottom and we're there. I saw the muddy trail we took years back as a shortcut on the way down to Agua Azul. We brought some picnic foods to have while spending the day. Agua Azul is so beautiful, all this green jungle and right in the middle is this blue water in a river! Well, this place has grown quite a bit since '87. Back then there was only a small restaurant and the white shell of a house. The house was still there along with several restaurants and shops. The water was still pretty as ever. The boys were quite impressed. You know it's one thing to see it on TV or a movie, but when you're there, it's nice. We wanted to get away from the crowds, so we walked on up the river. We crossed the bridge made of a huge stump that was in the movie "Predator." Soon we were further upriver at a nice spot for a picnic and swim. I told the guys that there are whirlpools, to be careful. We get in and swim to the middle of the river to some rocks just by some rapids. They wanted to jump in, but they would have to swim to the edge out of the current because there was a dropoff about twenty yards down river. Don and Evers both jumped in, and the current took them but then were able to swim out of the current to safety. Nathan was last and then he jumped, and he kept going, and going, finally I yelled, "Hey dude! You gonna swim or what?" Finally, he swam and avoided falling over a small waterfall. We got out and prepared some sandwiches. As we were eating, I noticed that some of the trees in the area had huge thorns. I pulled off some that looked like horns in a U shape. I put them in an empty cigarette pack and then in my backpack. We go back and browse through some of the shops they had. I think I bought a jaguar t-shirt. At the end of the day, we head back to Mayabell. We get ready to head to San Cristóbal. The plan is to stay two or three nights and just chill in the cool mountain town.

We head on to town and get our tickets at the second-class bus station. It's about five hours or so to get to San Cristóbal. It's a long bus ride, but we finally get there. The guys are once again impressed. It's nice, cool, and very picturesque being up in the mountains. I decide that I'll just go ahead and get our tickets since we were already at the bus station. Something came over me and I asked for tickets leaving the following day, rather than in two or three. I went back and told my peoples, and they were like "Why?" "I don't know," I said. So, we got a couple of rooms went out to eat and enjoy the sights. I was in the plaza talking to a local and he was interested in my opinions with regards to the NAFTA treaty which was going to go into effect in just a couple of days. I told them that it wouldn't be good for the campesino as it would raise prices on corn and other goods. The local agreed. Today's date is December 30. We walk down the main street to the crafts market, near the church. I think it's La Iglesia de Santo Domingo. It was a mustard yellow and reddish brown. Nathan wanted a pair of huaraches, Mexican sandals. They were of the area, with thick leather straps and a tire tread. I have a pair that I picked up on a previous trip, still have them. Well, he didn't have enough money, so I bought them for him. I told him that he could pay me later when we got back home. I had lent Don and Evers a little bit also. Those were such awesome kids. I'm proud of them. They've had such an awesome attitude the whole time. I was happy and proud to be a Spanish teacher. We did some shopping and head on to our hotel to wash up and change so that we can grab a bite and call it a night. I was able to get a route directly to Mexico City. Next thing I know it's New Year's Eve and we're at the Mexico City airport around 10:00 in the evening and hear on the news that roads leaving San Cristóbal have been blocked with overturned buses. It turns out that this was the beginning of the Zapatista uprising in southern Mexico. The NAFTA treaty was going to hurt many of the poor population. The farmers would not be able to make enough money since the price of corn had dropped quite a bit. I feel that we would have been in more danger from the Mexican troops than from the Zapatistas. We would have been prevented from leaving San Cristóbal for two weeks! Good thing we left when we did. Great trip!

14. Trip Six: 21st Century Palenque

I started thinking about doing another trip in the fall of 2007. At that time, I was divorced from my first wife and married to my second wife, Ladema. I had moved back to my hometown of Alice to help my dad during his retirement. I didn't want him living alone. I moved back in 2004 with Ladema, and her daughter, Megan, came to live with us. It was the fall of her senior year in '07 when I decided to do the trip. It would be during the Christmas break. Yeah, we would be spending Christmas in the jungle. Neither Ladema nor Megan had ever done anything like this before. I had taken Megan twice to Cozumel a couple of dive trips. I'll talk about those later in the book.

Besides Palenque, Agua Azul, and San Cristóbal, I had always wanted to visit the ruins of Tikal in Guatemala and Bonampak, Mexico, ever since I was an undergraduate student. I have told my wife about my previous adventures and she's up for adventure as well. By now we have already had several dive adventures in Cozumel. She has also grown very fond of Mexico, it's people and culture. I decide to fly out of San Antonio to Villahermosa and bus it from there, by far the best and quickest way to travel where we want to go. We would backpack it and travel light, no more huge backpacks, learned that after my first trip to Palenque.

We drive up to the airport in S.A. and use their parking. We walk from the parking lot to the airport terminal. As soon as we get there Megan realizes that she left her itouch iPod in the car. So, she runs to the car to retrieve it. We would have a short layover in Mexico City going and a longer one on our return trip. While waiting in line I struck up a conversation with some people who lived there in Mexico City. Since I had not been in Mexico City since the mid-

1990s I asked them if the best way to get to Chapultepec Park from the airport was the subway and they looked at me and said "No, no. Take a taxi the metro was way too dangerous." The last time I took the subway was in '91 with no problems at all. We board and take off to the D.F. and get there in a couple of hours, better than twenty-five hours. We spend an hour and a half before we take off for Villahermosa. It's early afternoon when we arrive. We take a taxi to our hotel, the Best Western Maya. It's nice. I'd never seen this part of Villahermosa. Megan needed to buy a swimsuit, so we walked down the road and crossed under an overpass where there was a Wal-Mart, believe or not. So, we walk in, and it is so packed inside with people making it difficult to walk. Besides that, it seemed that there was not much order in the store. I mean there were opened boxes full of clothes or whatever. It took a while before Megan found something. We then headed back to the hotel, on the way, as I just recently found out that someone had tried to take Megan's Nikes from her backpack. I did not know that had happened. I guess I was walking ahead of everyone and didn't notice. No one ever said anything to me about that. Then we stop at a little restaurant to get something to eat. I guess I ordered an extra set of tacos mistakenly. We ate them later at the hotel. Our plan was to get up early and head to the bus station. You could tell with the hotel motifs that we were in Maya land. I had never seen stained glass Maya art, very cool. Ladema and Megan decide to jump in the pool, but they didn't stay in it for too long. I thought it was a little too chilly for my bones. I'll have another opportunity to go swimming later.

15. Palenque and Mayabell

The following morning, we took a taxi from the hotel to the second-class bus station. I had only been to the first class one, but I was up for adventure. We get there and it's packed. I get our tickets and Ladema and Megan go for some coffee. I had been waiting for a while already when they walk up empty handed. They came and said that the lady at the counter had ignored them and never bothered to ask them for their order. So, I walk over to the counter and ask "Oiga señora, ¿Por qué no les tomó su ordén?" Lady, why did you not take their order? She answers, "Pues, no sabía que querían algo! I didn't know that they wanted something. Let me add, that my wife is a blond-haired blue-eyed beauty and was probably discriminated against. So, I order the three coffees myself and head back to the waiting room to sit. It's some of the nastiest coffee that I've ever had. I would have to wait until we got to Chiapas for an excellent cup of coffee. It's time to board so Ladema and I were able to get seats. Megan, on the other hand, had to stand for a while after giving up her seat to an elderly gentleman until there was a seat available. I felt proud of her for doing that. I had been telling them that Palenque was a little dusty town, at least it was the last time I was there. The bus ride takes a couple of hours. The first-class buses get there quicker. When you leave the state of Tabasco and come into Chiapas the landscape changes dramatically, especially when leaving the town of Palenque for the archaeological zone. We start pulling into Palenque and there are huge highways and hotels and all kinds of stuff. I was looking for the Mayan head statue at the entrance of the main drag there. I barely saw it for all the development and stuff. Now this was 2007 and there was a lot of interest in the Mayas because of the December 21, 2012, date. In town we grab a bite to eat and head to Mayabell so we take a colectivo. Before we leave, I notice a travel agency on the main drag. I didn't know when I was coming back to town, so I wanted to make reservations to get to Tikal and back. We get dropped off at Mayabell and walk up the driveway. The ceiba tree at the entrance was huge. It wasn't that big the last time I was here. I start to smell that old familiar smell and think, *Wow I'm home!* At the reception they said they now have cabañas in addition to the palapas. For the first couple of nights, we stayed in a cabaña, although I did bring my hammock.

The cabaña had a couple of beds a private shower with hot water, we were styling. The restaurant was now near the entrance by the reception. It used to be on the other side of the owner's house. You had to cross a causeway over the water. Now they had fixed up their pool and pool area with umbrellas and tables. It was very nice. The food at the restaurant is excellent and varied. The coffee is very good too, especially the café con leche! We go to our cabaña and drop off our backpacks before heading out to the ruins. As we're walking down the road, I'm thinking we'll take the back trail into the ruins. The old hotel opposite the road from the back trail entrance had been fixed up very nicely and was now a museum. Unfortunately, the trail was closed off and you can only come out the trail from the ruins. It was now only an exit and not a back entrance anymore. They even had security posted at the exit, making sure that no one came in that way. That meant we had some more walking to do. So, we continue about half a mile and the road curves to the left, to the main entrance of the park. For the first time in what was now my sixth trip, I paid to get into the park. It's not expensive at all, maybe a couple of dollars. I made sure to be in front of my wife and Megan as we were walking the trail to the ruins. I wanted to see their expressions. The trail is covered by big trees but then it opens up to the Temple of Inscriptions, and I see their expressions. As usual, mouths drop. It is so amazing to see these temples and pyramids in the midst of a tropical rain forest.

The Temple of Inscriptions is now closed to the public. You cannot climb up the pyramid anymore which means, you cannot go down to Pacal's tomb like before. On my previous trip with the boys, it had been closed as well. However, the smaller temple besides the Temple of Inscriptions, had been completely excavated. We were able to climb it and go inside. Nothing really to see. Even on my third trip the temple was completely covered. It is also prohibited to go up the tower. On all previous trips the tower was open. We went into the Palace Complex and went underneath to the labyrinth where before only priest and royals could enter. This is where the royals did their bloodletting ceremonies to communicate with the gods. Every time I come here, I am blown away by the beauty and awesomeness of this place. It's almost like one is in a dream, in a state of mind. We went into the courtyard of the Palace. There were big stone carvings. That was the end of the line for enemy captives.

On Christmas morning we had climbed the Temple of the Sun and just chilled with a view of the main plaza. For the first time in all my trips there were howler monkeys within the ruins. They were very close on the trees around the temples. I took pictures and some video of them. What a treat! It was amazing. We head on back to Mayabell via the back trail. We explored another complex of ruins on our way out. I think it was called the Bat Complex. We continued on our way; I saw that it was no longer possible to swim in the Queen's Bath. It was fenced off, and the trail was no longer muddy. They had added small rocks and pebbles and the trail now looked almost like a sidewalk. It was a nice upgrade. I remember getting all muddy and climbing our way up the hill using the roots of big trees to climb up. As we came out to the road, we crossed it and went into the museum. It was very nice, lots of artifacts of all sorts. We walked back to Mayabell and settled in for the evening. The cabaña had a fan to keep us cool. Before bed, Ladema and Megan wrote in their travel journals while I read my book, *I, Rigoberta..*

On all my trips we always meet cool and interesting people there at Mayabell. This time was no different. We met a couple of guys from California, Adam and Dan, and Dan's dog, Coyote. It's funny because in Alice, where I was presently teaching, our mascot was the coyote. I gave him one of my Alice Coyote t-shirts. It was very fitting. Megan had scored a couple of doobies from Dan. Like I said before, pot smokers always seem to find each other. We later took a walk in the jungle. The guys said that they had found a very cool spot that had natural pools of water. We took a hike and found the pool area very scenic. Palenque is surrounded by water and its good water at that. Even at the ruins, I would fill my water bottle from the faucet. It was clean and very cold. We got back to the campground and headed into town to make reservations to get to Tikal. At the travel agency the manager was nice and friendly. He even let me use some of their glue to use on my Reebok sandals. It didn't hold very well, and I ended up using zip ties to keep them together. In town we ate at a restaurant where they made their own homemade corn tortillas. It was like a mini tortillería. My wife was astounded. The excursion to Tikal, Guatemala, was only $39.00 U.S. one way, pretty good deal. It's been on my "must see" list since my undergraduate days.

16. Dusty Road to Flores, Sunrise in Tikal, Agua Azul

A couple of days later we get picked up at Mayabell and we head to Guatemala. We went back towards town before taking the highway out. After about a couple of hours, we pull into the Lacandón village of Nahá. It was about eight o'clock in the morning. There was a big palapa with long tables underneath where we would be eating. They had big tree stumps for seating. You could see the clouds in the forest, very cool. The bus would take us to the Mexican-Guatemalan border on the Usamacinta River at Frontera Corozal. There we get on these long and narrow boats to get us across. There was a couple from Germany who was carrying huge backpacks. It brought back memories. Well on the way we see women doing their laundry at the river's edge. They would beat the clothes on big rocks. The river ride was about an hour or so. We disembark and sit and wait for our bus to come pick us up. We waited for a while. Our bus shows up and we put our backpacks on top of the bus on racks. We travel a few miles to the Customs Office. Once there, I had to climb up on top of the bus to get the papers I needed. This place is kind of out in the country. Everyone is very quiet and solemn. We get our passports stamped and go back outside to wait for all the others. Soon we're all done and get back on the road. The road was long with the pavement ending soon after we took off. I get comfortable in my seat and begin to listen to my iPod. Yeah, no more cassette tapes! A couple of hours down the road I notice that there is dust coming into the bus. I shook my head a bit and all this dust starts flying all over the place. The dust was very fine, and I didn't want it to mess up my iPod so I kept it covered a bit more. The trip takes about five hours or just a bit more. We start pulling up into Flores. It's kind of like Tenochtitlán, an island in the middle of a lake. It was like that, only that it had one causeway in and out of Flores. First, we stop at a bank so that people could change some money. In Guatemala their dollar is called a quetzal, like the bird of paradise of the area. I had my earbuds in and the officer in the bank motioned me to remove them, so I did. We exchanged our money and went outside back to our bus. When we got outside the bus was gone! Fuck! Megan was on the bus and it was nowhere in sight! Our hearts skipped a few beats and we soon saw the bus returning. It had to move so it went around the block. When it got back Megan was looking at us through the window with a frown and Ladema got a pic of her! Whew!

The bus driver would now drive by some hotels for us to check in. Before we get off at the first hotel, we decided to get picked up at 3:00 A.M. to see the sunrise from atop a pyramid. Tikal was two hours from Flores. It was a very basic, no frills. The room was $17.00 U.S., cheap. I could have or should have waited for a better hotel, it's not like I couldn't afford it. We get to our room, and I needed a shower badly. The shower head had a switch to turn on for hot water. When I switched it on, I got shocked with electricity. There was an exposed wire going into the shower head. I managed to shower quickly. Ladema was the last to shower. She had managed to get all lathered up when suddenly, the water had cut off! I went back to the hotel reception and explained what had happened. The man working the front desk gave me a two-dollar discount for the room but, Ladema had to dry off with a towel. She still had soap in her hair and all over.

After we all showered, sort of, we went out to eat. We walked along the water's edge and found a café where we could look at the lake. We were going to be getting up very early so we wouldn't be out for too long. After eating Ladema and I like to "walk it off" and proceeded down the road. We stopped and bought some souvenirs and t-shirts. We went and looked around in one small store. They had clothing and stuff. The indigenous woman working there asked me if Ladema was my mother. Ladema understood what she had said, and said, "Oh hell no." Ladema grabbed me and pulled me out of the store without buying anything. Ladema said that she was "hitting" on me by insulting her. Oh well I was ready for bed.

Well, we didn't get too much sleep as it was two-thirty when we got up. We were waiting on the steps of the hotel by 3:00 A.M. I wore a long sleeve pullover and shorts. It was very chilly, almost cold. Soon enough the bus shows up and takes us to Tikal. Like I said it was a two-hour drive to Tikal, and we make it there by 5:00 A.M. It's very dark and we're the first ones there. The people working there told us to start walking the trail towards Pyramid V. It's a good way. We three are walking by ourselves. After walking for about ten minutes a small truck comes by and asks us if we want a ride. Of course, we do! In no time we're at the pyramid. There's a ramp on the side of the pyramid. There are trees and earth still on the pyramid, it hasn't been fully excavated. We make it to the top and it is chilly. After a while there's quite a crowd behind us. We sat at the front edge of the temple. It was still dark, and you could hear the howlers in the distance. As it's getting lighter all we can see is the fog, and soon the fog dissipates just enough to see the roof comb of Temple IV above the treetops! I was able to get a couple of shots. It still looked so cool. Maybe not as dramatic as the sun coming through, but still nice. I was finally in Tikal! I couldn't believe it. I've waited over twenty years to make this trip.

People started going down the ramp off of the pyramid. It was just after seven o'clock. Our guide took us all around the nearby area. Tikal is huge even though only ten percent of it has been excavated. Our guide was young guatemalteco. We were speaking Spanish to each other. He thought I was Mexican, at first. He asked if all the Mexicans say "órale," and I said, "órale huey," he said, "Sí sí." We laughed. All the guides are very knowledgeable and take great pride in their jobs. He left us around ten o'clock. We went walking all around, very tiring. We went to Temple IV where they have long ladders going up to a very thin edge once on top. I really wanted to go up this one, but there were too many people up there already. We took pics of it instead and would climb a different one. There was a rest area right in front of Temple IV where I struck up a conversation with one of the workers. I told him that I thought it was too dangerous to climb at this moment. He agreed. He was telling me that two weeks prior a young American kid was running and jumping all around. He said he thought that he may have been on drugs or something and fell down the pyramid to his death! Seeing something like that would surely ruin one's vacation. Hearing that almost made me feel a little nauseated. So, we rested a bit and headed towards the main plaza. On the way we saw squirrel monkeys running up in the trees and we also saw a flock of toucans! Beautiful! At the main plaza we all climbed up Temple II or Temple of the Masks. Ladema and Megan went first. I stayed behind to take some pictures. There was a cement circle in front of Temple I or Temple of the Great Jaguar with a shaman making an offering and I guess, praying for the world. I went across the plaza to climb Temple II. Temple I and Temple II, both face each other at opposite ends of the main plaza. Very famous pyramids. My wife and I lost count, not that we were counting, how many times we've seen them on TV. It was starting to get hot, and we were tired. We headed to our bus around 12:00 P.M. and headed back to the border. The bus ride back wasn't as long nor as dusty. We made it to Customs and proceeded to exit the country. We crossed the Usamacinta and boarded our van at Frontera Corozal. Bonampak was nearby and I asked the driver if we could make a quick stop. Of course, he said "No podemos." "We can't." That was another trip. I'm still hopeful. Maybe take Holly and Audrey next time.

We make it back to Palenque and they take us back to Mayabell. What a trip! We're able to get a cabaña for the next couple of nights. The following day we decide to take a dip in the pool. I can't believe they have a pool. Ladema went in first and screamed. It was freezing. I confirmed it when I jumped in. Oh my, muy frío. The absolute coldest pool ever, even colder than Barton Springs Pool in Austin.

We met a woman who was living in Mayabell for a few months. She was an older woman, short of stature, who was an artisan, named Calypso. I met her on a previous trip. She didn't remember, but I did. How do you forget the name Calypso? Well Megan had decided to sleep outside in Calypso's palapa in a hammock. She said that she was going straight over there to Calypso's. We decided to walk her there so that she wouldn't get lost.

Earlier that day we went into town to make reservations for Agua Azul. It's about a couple of hours or so. The guy at the travel agency recommended that we try the "mojarra empapelada." It's a fish. So, the next day they came to pick us up at Mayabell. On the way we stop at the Misol Ha waterfalls. It's kind of tall, but small. Nothing like Agua Azul. We walk around behind the falls and try not to get wet from the spray. The hike back is uphill to get back to the colectivo. We get back on the road with Ladema and Megan in the front seat. The driver was hauling ass and we soon get to the crucero and hang a right. The road winds down. I see the muddy trail shortcut that we took on my second trip. We get there and I cannot recognize the place. There are restaurants and shops everywhere, many of them. I recognize the falls. The water is still amazing as ever. I remember getting a coconut ice cream cone. This one little kid asked me for some. I took one last lick, and he took it from me. Next, I tried some salted banana chips. I couldn't believe how good they were. We look around and find a restaurant to eat. We all order the "mojarra." They bring it to you head and all. Megan and Ladema had to cover the head to be able to eat it. It was very good. Afterwards we walk upriver a bit away from all the crowds and Megan and I go in for a little dip. The water is cool. The old white house is still there. I remember when that was one of two buildings here at Agua Azul. It was very dilapidated and practically falling apart. Past the house was only jungle. Progress? Who knows? It's time to leave and head to the where the van is parked. We need to use the facilities before we go. There's a little kid, maybe ten years old who oversees collecting the money. It's not much, a couple of pesos, but I only had very large denominations of pesos. I did have a dollar. I told him that it was worth way more than two pesos, but he wouldn't take it and would not allow us to use the restroom. There's a building across the road from the restrooms and I tell the man that the kid won't take a dollar for us three. The man comes out and chews him out. At last, he relents and takes the dollar. Shit, what a hassle.

On the way back both Ladema and Megan refuse to sit in the front seat. They got scared on the way to Agua Azul because of the chauffeur's driving. We all sat on the second row in the van. Some of the other travelers on the van offered us some tiny bananas. They were soo good and creamy. The driver was going to drop a lady off somewhere along the way back. About halfway to Palenque we stop in the middle of the country to wait for the woman's ride. We waited and waited. It was getting dark. We stopped in the middle of a palm date orchard. Huge date palm trees everywhere. I have to take a walk way off the road to take a leak. I think everyone was just about ready to start heading back to Mayabell. We would be heading back in a couple of days to Villahermosa early so that we could go visit Parque La Venta. We stayed in a different and bigger cabaña. It was towards the swimming pool. It was like a duplex with a shared patio. That first night back it rained very hard. I had never seen it rain that hard in Palenque before. I'm glad we were indoors. We went back to the ruins to spend the day. We're all still as amazed to see all of this now as we were the first time we saw it. We all stayed in a palapa that final night. Ladema and I shared a hammock and it seemed that we "rocked" the palapa a bit too much for Megan's liking and she went to sleep in Calypso's palapa.

17. PARQUE LA VENTA AND MEXICO CITY

It was time to begin our journey back. We took a colectivo back to Palenque early and went to the bus station where we boarded a bus for Villahermosa. We got to Villahermosa and walked to the same hotel we stayed at before. We checked in quickly and set out for Parque La Venta. I had always wanted to see the giant Olmec heads. It was a small park. There were a couple of caged jaguars. It was sad to see them like that. We walked a trail where the heads and other artifacts were. All kinds of stone carvings and figures. We kept hearing noises in the undergrowth of the area. Down the trail the coatimundis started coming out of the bushes and onto stone tables and monuments. I didn't know what they were at the time. It was only until later when I looked it up and found out. We went into the small museum after walking the trail and we saw the famous figurines of the Olmec elders gathered in a circle. Pretty cool. We headed back to the hotel. We left early to Mexico City the following morning and we would have a few hours to sight see. We were at the airport and walked to take the Metro, the subway. It was twenty cents to take it across town to Chapultepec Park. It was clean and not many people. I saw where we had to get off. There was a little kid going our way and he made sure we would get off at the right stop. We walked over to the Museo Nacional de Antropología and since it was a Monday and December 31 it was closed. I was so disappointed. I was looking forward to it but, what can you do? I languished for a moment, then we caught a taxi to the Zócalo. I thought that we could go and see the Templo Mayor. Well, like I said before, it was Monday, and it was also closed. We took some pictures, Megan got a "limpiada," a cleansing from an indigenous shaman. It was a happening place. There were all these danzantes aztecas, Aztec dancers, dancing there in the Zócalo by the old church. We went inside the National Cathedral, and it is so vast. Ladema could not believe how huge it was. There were like all these chapels all along the side of the cathedral. They were even trying to have mass with all these tourists around. There was like a large bit hanging from the ceiling to track how far it is sinking. It has sunk quite a bit. We then walked across the Zócalo to the Palacio Nacional, Mexico's equivalent to the White House in Washington. We gave our information upon entering and then it opens up to an indoor courtyard. All along the inside walls were the famous murals of Diego Rivera. He had painted the history of Mexico along the walls so that people who could not read nor write could go there and see it for themselves. It was magnificent! I couldn't believe it. I had seen some sections of it in books or films but seeing it person was quite awesome. I took quite a few pictures, and they even had a paper máché of Diego and Frieda. After a couple of hours, we went out back to the Zócalo. Lots of people getting ready to celebrate New Year's Eve. I felt lucky to be there, bringing in the New Year in one of the largest cities in the world. The Christmas decorations were all still up. This was my second time being in Mexico City on New Year's Eve. It was time to head on to the aeropuerto. We took a taxi and got there in no time. The airport was easy to maneuver, not like Houston, ugh. Soon I was driving to Alice from San Antonio still high from the trip! It was almost midnight. We got home just before midnight. Another awesome trip, I am so lucky. Will there be another trip so that I can visit Bonampak? I sure hope so…

PART TWO:

My Island Cozumel

❖

18. FIRST TRIP DEC. 1984, 1985– 1989 THE LEAN YEARS

I had earned my Bachelor's degree in the summer of '84. That summer my girlfriend, at the time, and I took scuba diving. We both received our P.A.D.I. Open Water and Advanced Open Water certifications while students at Southwest Texas State University. I would begin teaching first-year Spanish while attending graduate school. I was offered the teaching fellowship at the university, and I could not believe it. Just before the beginning of the fall semester there was a big barbeque for the faculty at the university's president's house, it was President Hardesty. It was cool rubbing elbows with former and future professors. I went with my friend Javier, who was also on the Department of Modern Languages faculty. He was working on his Ph.D. out of UT Austin. We've since lost touch but we had some good times. At that time I was living out in the country north of San Marcos. I lived in a cottage where I worked for my rent. My rent was work for fourteen hours a week. Pretty good deal for me at the time. Vanessa had moved in with me for a short while living in my trailer. I saw an ad for this place and was able to get it. We both moved in together in the summer of '83 and now in the summer of '84 she was ready to move out and I was going to help her find a place. It was amicable and I was soon teaching at the university. I loved it. I attended graduate school studying Spanish and Psychology. I was twenty-three years old, single, and looking for adventure. The Dive Shop was advertising a trip to Cozumel just after Christmas and a few days past New Year's. The trip was round-trip airfare from Houston, 7 nights hotel, 5 days of diving, with lunch, one night dive, and a beach party, all for $495.00! Can you believe it? That was so cheap compared to today's prices. I still wanted to learn more about diving. I met quite a few people through

71

diving. Divers are some of the coolest people around. There were just over one hundred people signed up for the trip, which meant that we would be flying charter. It was a party on the plane. In '84 people were still allowed to smoke. There was a cloud of smoke in the plane! People started throwing me their barf bags when they found out it was my first trip on a jet. I was feeling the love. We would all be staying in different hotels in the downtown area there in San Miguel. I would be staying at El Marquéz and my roommate was a guy named Andy. I became friends with Don Jorge's son, Daniel. He worked the reception area. They also sold beer, which was very convenient for us. While I was unloading all my gear, I heard someone call my name. Craig, my dive instructor came looking for me. He needed me to do some translating at a different hotel. So, there I go "el profesor" to straighten things out and I don't mind at all. After smoothing out the room situation, I am yet called a few times more and to be on call if needed. No problem, life was good. We got ready to go to the other side of the island for a welcome party. There were quite a few vehicles. After all, there were just over a hundred people on the trip and getting the logistics right was important. Cozumel is about twenty-one miles long and around twelve miles wide. We would take the "transversal" which was the main road that crossed the island, near the middle part. We would be going to the windward side of the island where the undertow is very strong. Back then just about straight ahead just as the paved road turned to the right is where we stopped. It was all beaches. There was a coral cup with a small path to it where people took pictures. There was also a small cave, called "la Cueva del Amor," Love Cave. Several years later a hurricane changed the beach and no more coral cup or cave. It's hopping these days with Mescalito's. It's a very cool place to have a cold one with some ceviche. That would be years later. Back to this first trip, there was an instructor who was working at The Dive Shop, I can't remember his name, but he had short hair, wore glasses, and was a bit of an asshole. Anyway, he brought along a Tekna underwater scooter. They got the scooter out of the truck. It was in a big black plastic case. Well, that guy put on his mask, fins, and snorkel and proceeded to get into the water. The waves were breaking almost right on shore. Now I assumed that he had been here before as had most of the instructors working at The Dive Shop. He gets in and the waves suck him and the scooter out to sea. He loses everything and was lucky to make it back out alive. I mean he wasn't much more than about five feet out from the shore. I'm guessing that he hadn't been to Cozumel before. So why hadn't any of the other instructors try to talk him out of it? Perhaps they did try. He was the type of guy who thinks they know best, more than anyone. Other than that, we went down the beach and snacked. Seeing blue water changed my life. I needed it more and more. Hard to explain. We headed on back. Now there was a sand / dirt road to the left of where we were that runs north along the coastline. Rental car agencies prohibit cars from going on that road as they could get stuck or worse. Although we had a trip planned down that road later in the trip. There was a Mayan temple on the far northeast shore called "El Castillo."

We made it back to town it was starting to get dark, and I was getting hungry. Our hotel, El Marquéz, is a block from the town square. They have music and dances every Saturday night where all the locals and tourists get together. Andy, my roommate, walked down the street away from the plaza to find a place to eat. We found a small taqueria and I ordered some tacos. I asked the guy working there if the salsa was picante, and he said, "Nah." I proceeded to put some on all the tacos. I took a bite, and my mouth was on fire. I kept eating because I was hungry. After that first bite, I couldn't taste my food! It was a habanero sauce. I was young only 24 years old, what do you expect? Just a little taste test would have prevented that fire. I wanted to turn in so that tomorrow could come. I had all this desire just from watching *"The Undersea World of Jacques Cousteau."* Most recently watching slide shows from other divers only got me more pumped up to do it.

We all came together the following morning, a couple of blocks away at another hotel. Easier to let everyone know what boat they will be on. The street in front of El Marquéz was a functioning street. Later, they would close it to motor vehicles, to make it more pedestrian friendly. I remember seeing Bill Horn, owner of Aqua Safari, trying to get everyone where they needed to be. Aqua Safari's dive shop is on the malecón, Rafael Melgar is the street closest to the water. Their pier is right across the street.

For two tanks and buffet lunch they charged $36.00 U.S. We all walk to the Aqua Safari pier in town which is very convenient. I was on the boat Ocean 1 with my instructor Craig. I liked the people on our boat, but then again, most divers are cool people. We would do our deep dive first. I remember diving Santa Rosa Reef and my buddy Andy decided to just keep going deeper, too deep. I then see Craig swim by me hauling ass to catch him. I don't know what the hell Andy was thinking, but I sure as hell wasn't going to save him on my very first ocean dive. Whew! That was a close one. I knew then that I needed to learn more. I could not be his dive buddy anymore. I stayed away from him underwater. After that dive we head on to San Francisco beach for our surface interval and have a buffet lunch, a game of volleyball or just chilling for a while, minus the alcohol of course. Our divemaster was Sergio. Everyone on our boat pitched in on our last day for a good tip. Craig and Sergio were friends. I knew to stay with Sergio since he knew where all the cool sea life lay. The thing about Aqua Safari, although an excellent dive operation, their boats are slow and it takes forever, about an hour and a half to get to some of the deeper reefs south of the island on the leeward side. On the way to our first dive site, I saw flying fish. It was so cool. Seeing the different shades of blue the water was mesmerizing. Our boat was low to the water, so I did my first back roll into the ocean. It was all blue. This was what I had waited for all my life. It was like, I was home. I'm so glad that I got certified to dive and I still wanted to learn more. We were at Palancar Caves, and I stayed with Sergio, he led me through a swim through and when I came out, I saw what was to be the largest spotted eagle ray I will have ever seen. It swam a couple of feet above my head. It had to be about seven feet across. I was lucky to be there. There were barracudas and these colorful little reef fish. There were spotted moray eels, angelfish, grey, french, and queen. I saw the native to Cozumel splendid toad fish and peacock flounder. So many cool creatures. On one of our dives one guy pulled what he thought was black coral. He stuck it in his bc jacket pocket. A little bit was sticking out and touching the inside of his arm. He kept turning around and he finally took it out and tossed it. I think it was sea nettle. It looks black, so he figured that it was black coral. In Cozumel black coral was very popular. There are jewelry shops that sold it and many other shops as well. It grows very deep.

We do our deep dive and afterwards head to the beach for lunch. There were all these other boats there for lunch as well. It was so cool to be a part of all this. We go through a buffet line, and I get a piece of what I thought was beef. I later found out it was turtle. Back then they weren't protected, turtles that is. They sold turtle lotion that was very popular. After eating and playing a few games of volleyball we head on out for our shallow dive. It was around 1:00 P.M. when we head out. I think we probably went to Paradise Reef. It is closer to town. After we finish diving it's about 4:00 P.M. when we get back to our room. Later during the trip, we would do two night-dives as well. We would be going out to Carlos N Charlie's later that evening for drinks. Carlos N Charlie's also had great food, especially "los huesitos," the ribs. At that time in Cozumel the popular clubs were Neptuno's and Scaramouche. Everyone was partying and having a great time. My friend Randy knew Jimmy, the owner of Carlos N Charlie's. He gave us a couple of buckets of Corona beer which we gratefully guzzled down. We spend New Year's there at Carlos N

Charlie's. They gave us styrofoam balls to throw at each other at midnight. There were ceiling fans all over and I reached up to catch one of the balls being thrown and the fan caught my hand pretty good. On the trip I met Paul, who was also an instructor, he let me know that he was looking for a couple of divemasters to help him with his classes at the university. I told him that I was indeed interested in continuing my dive education. I did work with him the following semester. Prior to going to Carlos N Charlie's on New Year's Eve we did a night dive, my first one in the ocean. It was very memorable since there was a full moon that was clearly visible under fifty feet of water! This was quite amazing and a great experience. A couple of nights later we did another night dive. It was rainy and we had a big group on the "Karla." It was a big old wooden blue boat. We had to do a giant stride to get into the water and it was a high drop down to the water. It was getting rough. Underwater was no problem but getting out of the water and back into the boat was very tricky. The boat had a ladder on the side and the boat would rise quite high with the swells of the waves. You had to time it when the boat was coming down you had to be able to grab the ladder and climb up. We had to remove our fins before attempting this. It was a very stormy night and for a big group of people with no accidents we were lucky.

On the two days that we did not dive we did a couple of excursions, one to the San Gervasio Mayan ruins and a picnic down the sand road alongside the northeast coast to El Castillo. It was a long road getting to the San Gervasio ruins. They were located around the center of the island about halfway down the transversal road. In ancient times the Mayans did pilgrimages to San Gervasio since there was a shrine to the fertility Goddess Ixchel. The ruins were quite small, but these were the first that I had seen. Some of the building still had the original paint. Make sure that you bring mosquito repellent because they sure do get thick. We spend around an hour there and head on to our next adventure. We continue down the transversal road to the other side of the island, but rather than staying on the pavement to the right, we turn left down the sand road. We travel for over an hour when we eventually get there. We followed one another in a caravan. There was one temple there and it was tall. It was El Castillo. There were already some people there. There were even a few on top of El Castillo. I thought, *well shit, I want to climb it too.* I looked at the wall and just started climbing find bumps and niches where to put my hands and feet. I get to the top and climb up. I raise my hands like I'm the king of the world. Then this one guy asks me, "Hey are you a rock climber?" I said "No." I then realized that I would have to climb back down. Oh, oh, I thought to myself. He saw my worried face and told me that I could always climb back up if I had to. Well, I just wanted to enjoy the view for a little while longer before I had to think about climbing down. It was an awesome view from where I stood atop El Castillo. I know Tulum and Chichén both have an "El Castillo." The one I was on wasn't as high as those two. It was still between thirty and forty feet high. I thought about jumping off but, it was just too high for me to think that I wouldn't get hurt. It was the moment of truth, and I was really nervous. I lay down parallel to the edge. I let my right foot go over the edge and I was looking for a foothold. As soon as I found a secure place to put my foot, I just continued pulling my body over the edge very carefully. As soon as I got my body over the edge it seemed very easy to climb back down, no problem. Thinking about it was way worse. This would be the first and last time that I would be at this part of the island on twenty-six trips and counting.

One afternoon some of us went down to the beach at the Sol Caribe hotel. Waiters came out onto the beach and would take our orders. Out in the water, near the International Pier is a sunken plane. It was put there for a movie in the 70's and a decent dive. We dove it a couple of times. A few years later, my brother Adrian and my then-wife Laura did a night dive there. By that time the plane was mostly covered by sand.

Back at the hotel there was another guy who worked there named César. He had a motorcycle and he let me drive it around town for a bit. It was cool of him. He later worked for the rental agency Thrifty. Also, on this trip we met a taxi driver named José Luis. He was so cool as well. He asked me what my nationality was, I told him that I was a Tejano. He thought that I was from somewhere up north in Mexico. He said I that I had a norteño accent. I told him that I was a Chicano. He looked at me a little shocked. He said Chicano? I said, "Sí, méjico-americano." Chicano has more of a cultural pride thing, and it has less syllables. He then asked if I was in a street gang? I said, "Look at me!" I told him that I think he meant "pachuco." A young Mexican-American youth in street gangs between the 1930s to the 50s. Anyway, Jose Luis drove us around wherever we needed. We fed him too. We had asked him if he could score us some weed and gave him a $20.00 U.S. He came back to our hotel an hour later with a trash bag full of weed. Not completely full, but about a quarter of it. It was at least a quarter of a pound, but probably closer to half a pound. It was a lot of weed. It was like the scene straight out the movie "Club Paradise" before it came out. We almost finished it and had to give away what we could not finish smoking, probably about an ounce. We would see each other on subsequent trips in the following years. José Luís gave me a black coral joint holder. It had been carved. That was so cool of him to do. There was a toga party that started in a hotel and ended up at Carlos N Charlie's. Everyone went, it was so much fun. One of the girls flashed everyone a few times, oh yeah! My biggest disappointment was not seeing a shark. I would see my first shark the next summer in Jamaica. It was the biggest nurse shark that I would ever see. It was around eight or nine feet long. It was laying still in a shallow cave on Silver Spray reef. I was hooked.

I traveled to Cozumel ten times from 1984 to 1989. On the last day of this first trip to Cozumel, Randy and I came across two Scuba

Pro regulators right there on the sidewalk and there was no one in sight. We walked it over to Discover Cozumel Diving and gave them to Tomás and Miguel, two of their divemasters. This would set us up for a few trips of low-cost diving. On my following trips we would meet Miguel and or Tomás, to let them know we were ready to dive. They would pick us up at a hotel or we would leave from their pier. Discover had a very nice boat called the *Caribbean Princess*. It was styling with cushions all over the boat and air conditioning in the main cabin. I had taken three girls diving with them, two were girlfriends and one was just a friend. Rather than pay the dive shop, we would just pay the divemasters and the captains were cool about it.

One day I called Continental Airlines to find out how much airfare was to Cozumel, and it was $119.00 U.S. roundtrip! I made a reservation for the following day. There were several spur-of-the moment trips. On one of these early trips, Randy and I decided to dive with Deportes Acuáticos with Sergio, not the one from Aqua Safari. We would be diving Maracaibo to look for sharks! At last, we would be looking specifically for sharks. We left early on a smaller and much faster boat than those of Aqua Safari. It was four of us on the dive, Sergio, his camera man, Randy, and me. I enjoy and prefer diving with smaller groups. Maracaibo reef is the southernmost reef ice most likely to see the big sea creatures. We were in the mid-level water column with the reef starting around one-hundred and twenty feet. In about eighty feet of water, I saw three figures in the deep water, perhaps another eighty feet down. They started moving towards us. Three bull sharks, a five-, six-, and seven-footer. They came to check us out. When they got right up close to us a few feet away, the cameraman took a pic and another one as they turned around. It was such an adrenaline rush. From that moment I was (*definitely*) hooked on sharks.

Randy and I were staying at El Marquéz and find out that there is a strip club just down the block from the hotel. It was called "Jomans." I wondered just how good the club would be. Not many women, but the star attraction came up on the stage a proceeded to "smoke" a cigarette with her vajayjay. What? Yep, you could see the cigarette light up when she "inhaled." Well, I guess it was better than nothing.

Another year I took the girl I was dating. I taught her to scuba dive in her family's pool. It was another seven-night vacation with five days of diving. On our night dive I had borrowed Paul's Aqua Mini Sun. It was a normal night dive when suddenly, the currents shifted and took me and my girlfriend in the opposite direction as everyone else. We carried on as I really was paying more attention to the sea life. I didn't notice that there weren't any more divers around, we were just about out of air and decided to ascend to the surface. We came up and it was pitch black on the surface. We were far from shore and no boats around. I turned my light out and started doing the *Jaws* song and my girlfriend started hitting me pissed off and scared as hell. I told her to calm down and that they would not leave us out here. If worse came to worse, we could always try to swim to shore. I shined that light waving it around. I could barely see a light very far away. I kept shining the light and could then see a boat getting closer. It came up to us, but it wasn't our boat. Fuck! They offered to give us a ride, but I politely said, no. The captain said that he would radio our boat, the Princess. We thanked him and waited about fifteen more minutes before we got picked up. The divemaster knew exactly what had happened, currents. I was ready for a cold one!

Later that same trip, I did manage to take a ferry to Playa del Carmen and a colectivo to Tulum. It was very hot. I got queasy on the ferry. The heat was making me sick to my stomach. I dreaded the ferry ride back. I quit seeing that girl as soon as we got back. She was a little cray-cray. I also went on a trip with my brother and friend, Javier. We always have so much fun in Cozumel. It's tradition to rent a car at least on one of the days that we're there and go around the island stopping at Mescalito's for a Dos XX and ceviche, I wish I was there now.

19. MY AQUA SAFARI INTERNSHIP SUMMER OF '90

It was the spring of 1990 and I had just completed my course work for my Master's degree. All I had left was to do my internship. For my internship I had to go to a foreign country of the language that I was studying, Spanish. It was a no brainer that I would be going to Mexico since it was the closest country to where I was living at the time, Texas. I had choices. I could enroll in a university and take formal classes while living with a family. Or I could get a job and live with a family and write a twenty-chapter book of the experience. I felt confused about what to do. I thought that I would go and live with the Lacandón Indians of Nahá in Chiapas. My plan was to do this in the upcoming summer. It would be the rainy season in southern Mexico. I wasn't sure what to do. I was getting frustrated, and I told my mother that I was quitting college and that the degree was only a piece of paper. I was so frustrated. I ended up talking with Dr. Carlisle and he did a good job of talking me out of going to Chiapas. It would be a bit more complicated than the weather, getting permission from the village chief, etc.

I prayed to God to let me find the place to do my internship and took a drive in the country. I rolled a couple of doobies to grease the creative process. Well shortly into the drive the "weed of wisdom" had given me an obvious answer, Cozumel. I was already familiar with the island, its ways, and people. I was already a certified P.A.D.I. divemaster and could get a job. I got in touch with Bill, the owner of Aqua Safari, the oldest and best reputable dive shop in Cozumel. I had not dived with Aqua Safari since my very first trip back in '84. I wrote a letter to Bill telling him of my plans. I mentioned that I needed to do an internship, that I was a certified divemaster, and that there would be no monetary renumeration, I would work for free for six weeks. Hell, I was willing to sweep the floors if I had to. Anyway, my family is an RCI member and had three weeks of availability to their resorts at that time. I had always liked the layout and atmosphere of the Sol Caribe Hotel, now Park Royal. I made reservations to stay there for three weeks and the other three weeks I would stay at El Marquéz downtown. A couple of weeks later a got an answer from Bill at Aqua Safari. He gladly welcomed my proposition. He said that my work would be two-fold. For the first three weeks I would dive with the competition, working as a spy. Then I would work with Aqua Safari, assisting their divemasters. Soon I would meet with my committee chairman at the university, Dr. Champion. I told him of my plans, and he just smiled and asked, "You're going to work in Cozumel as a divemaster?" I think he wished it could have been he who was going. I would be staying in Cozumel for six weeks, but I had very little money and I did not want to ask my father for it. He would have gladly given it. My girlfriend, Laura, was living with me and she offered me $1000 to help me. She would go and stay with me for the first two weeks, then return to Texas. My brother, Adrian, would meet us in Cozumel after the first week. He and a friend would be there for the second week. My mother and Carlos would also visit during my fourth week. I would be staying at the resort Sol Caribe on my first, second, and fourth weeks there and the other three weeks I would stay in town at the El Marquéz hotel.

Upon arriving, I met with Bill from Aqua Safari. We had to come up with a checklist that I would use for my data collection that showed what type of operation each dive company had at the time. There was no uniform policy nor regulations that dive operators followed. This was to get all dive operators on the same page.

Earlier that spring, there was an episode of "Inside Edition" that brought to attention that a diver or two had gotten embolisms from diving in Cozumel with some people who had a boat and some tanks. These types of operations cannot handle life-threatening emergencies involved in scuba diving. Cozumel is a diving community that now had a lot of negative publicity due to the episode on "Inside Edition." It's hard when livelihoods are threatened. Later in the summer there would be a conference with the dive operators of Cozumel and Mexico's Secretary of Tourism.

Bill told me that he had done this several years earlier with a friend of his and thought that it would be a good idea to do it now with all that had happened recently.

I thought that it was good timing for my sake and long overdue for the people of and visitors to Cozumel. Bill and I collaborated on a type of dive analysis form. It would include the name of the dive shop, the price, the amount of dive masters or instructors on each dive, and what type of certifications they had. It included how many divers per dive guide they would be responsible for. How much they got compensated, salary, daily, weekly, etc.

I noted if the dive guides gave detailed briefing before the dive. This would include safety protocol, knowledge and layout of the reefs, conservation, and if they were friendly. Also included was if they had dropped onto a group and what their language skills were like. It is also important to note if the guides watched the divers. We tried to be as thorough as possible. There was a section for equipment, for example, if the tanks were all within five years of being hydrostatically tested, yearly visible inspection, fully filled to 3000 psi and by whom, first-aid kit, oxygen, functioning radio, clean boat, and type of engine. Bill and I did work on the document a couple of times adding to it. I also wrote notes on the back of each dive analysis form to include any pertinent information not included in the dive analysis form.

Once we were ready to begin, I would arrive early at Aqua Safari and would meet with Donna. She would give me cash for both Laura and I to dive and what dive shop to visit that day. This was so, so cool of Bill to do, to pay for Laura's diving as well. Laura and I just acted like regular dive tourists. Although I was always talking, to the divemasters, the captain or the divers themselves. I was trying to get as much information as possible. After a couple of weeks there was soon talk of a diver going around and asking all these questions. All in all, most of the dive shops ran good dive operations, but there was one that really stuck out and not in a good way.

It was an afternoon dive on a small boat, only two other divers besides Laura and me. The divemasters gave no briefing nor instructions and smelled strongly of alcohol. Once we got down, the divemaster disappeared and the couple looks at us with "saucer eyes." I motioned for them to stay with us and got them to give me the okay sign. When we came up, the divemaster was already in the boat waiting for us! That's pretty messed up. The dive shop was Dive Paradise. I did mention this story to the Secretary of Tourism at the conference at La Ceiba Hotel. I only mentioned the story but did not name the dive shop. That was in 1990, it is now 2021, I hope they've improved by now. I mentioned that most of the dive operators were doing a good job keeping divers safe, but a few needed much improvement. After the conference I was walking out of the building and there was a group of operators in the doorway. One called out to me and told me that I had just opened up a can of worms. "Lo siento mano," I told him. I did this for three weeks. The week after Laura had returned home, I was diving with Caribbean Divers, and met a young diver from San Antonio. I can't remember his name, but he attended John Jay High School. This was where my former football head coach had moved to after being in Alice. We had a good laugh and told stories to each other. After diving we went out on the town and partied a bit. Another time, we were picking up some divers at Plaza Las Glorias and I see Eric, one of my friends from San Marcos. Eric was just as surprised to see me. He was with his new girlfriend, Stacy. I told Eric about my internship. Eric is such a cool guy. Smiles a lot, just a good decent person. I got my two dogs from him, Alex, and Max. Well needless to say I spent some time with them while they were in Cozumel. They invited me for lobster! When it was time for them to leave, he leaves me with several joints that he couldn't finish. How freaking cool is that? I remember when Randy and I woke his ass up at three o'clock in the morning when he lived in Dallas, and he didn't even get pissed off. What a guy!

There was also this couple who were videographers working with Tony Tate's Underwater Video. They went on many of the dives with Aqua Safari. I think they dove for free or got a discount. They were super-friendly, and they did a good job. I bought a VHS cassette for $60 U.S. It included a turtle, porcupine pufferfish, spotted moray, a bunch of angelfish and a huge green moray eel named, la Güerita. Named by Charro, the Dundee of the Sea!

On one evening we did a night dive at the airplane. It was my brother Adrian, Laura, and myself. We all had lights and cyalume or "glow" sticks. The octopus that we saw was bluish but would change to orange. It was trying to get away from us and I tried to pick it up with my bare hands. It caught on to my hand and started sucking its way up my arm! Fuck! I hate that feeling! It was my own fault, I admit. We saw a parrotfish making its bubble for the night. They blow out saliva that forms a bubble around them and they sleep in there at night. When another fish bumps into the bubble they turn away. At the end of our dive, we cut open our glow sticks of blue, red, and yellow. We shook them good to get the liquid out, it's non-toxic, and then turned off our lights. Ooh. It looked like we were floating in space. It was so cool.

The next part of my internship was helping out Aqua Safari's divemasters. It's always been amazing to me how boat captains can identify what reef they are at. Take for example, Palancar. It's not one reef, but a complex of reefs, whether it's the Caves, the Gardens, the Horseshoe, etc. The Horseshoe used to have a statue, the "Christ of the Deep," with it's out-stretched arms, that is until Wilma came along. I had to work on my breathing since I would be one of the first in the water and the last one out. I was sucking those tanks nearly dry. After doing so much diving, I could equalize simply by exaggerating my swallowing. I no longer had to pinch my nose. I was so happy, being able to dive for free and logging sixty-four dives! Sometimes the divers would give me cash as a tip, but I always gave it to the divemaster or boat captain. I never kept a tip. On my final dive, just as I was ready to ascend, I look around then I look up and catch a glimmer of something in the sand. I go back down to the bottom and blow away some sand with my hand and I pulled up a gold Tag Heuer watch! When I came up on the boat, I showed the other divemaster and he asked me, "¿Me lo regalas? He asked, If I would "gift" it to him. I told him that he was crazy. We both laughed. I would end up gladly giving it to my girlfriend, Laura. It was appraised for $975.00 U.S.!

In the evenings at El Marquéz, I became good friends with the manager on night duty. He gave me quite a bit of information. I talked to the maids and to other Mexican nationals who were visiting Cozumel. I had to write on twenty different subjects or topics per chapter. I wrote about the reefs, the concept of time, superstitions, the differences, and similarities of American, European, and Mexican tourists. Also included were hotel zones, eating establishments, law enforcement, festivals, the protection of marine turtles, local sports, and religions. And of course, I included my job at Aqua Safari. Of all the people I had spoken with about their internships, mine I think was the best of all.

20. RETURN TO COZUMEL

It was now 2002 and I have been working on getting my life back on track after my divorce in 2001. My best friend, Louie, and I had been talking about going on a trip. He was newly divorced as well. In our conversations I had been talking about diving and about how cool it was. He got certified! Awesome! Now I had a dive buddy to dive with. We had talked about going to Amsterdam, but at the time he nor I had the funding for that trip, but we both could afford a trip to Cozumel. I now only had my basic scuba gear, mask, fins, and snorkel. I had an extra pair of fins that I let Louie borrow. I just needed to get into the blue. It had been twelve years since I had been to Cozumel, and this would be my twelfth trip. We booked a Funjet package for seven nights and five days of diving. We stayed at Casa Mexicana on the main drag, the malecón. I had never stayed there before, it was nice. Our diving was booked with Black Shark Dive Shop. The diving was good as usual. We rented a Jeep to go around the island, a tradition for me. One afternoon we went to San Francisco Beach and rented some wave runners. It was full throttle the whole time. It was like being in a linebacker position with bent knees leaning a little forward. We were so sore the next few days we could barely walk. All in all, it was a great trip and it felt good to be back. One night we did go to the Caribbean Queen strip club on the transversal road just at the edge of town. We just had a few beers and headed back to the hotel for the night. I will always be thankful for Louie. We go way, way back to when we were children, he's my brother, and I love that guy!

In the spring of 2003, I met my current wife. She too got certified and was quite afraid of the water as well. I must give her credit for having the courage to face her fear, it's not an easy thing to do. She had never been to Cozumel before and had only visited border towns of Mexico, like Nuevo Laredo and Matamoros that are across the Texas border. On this trip I still had no gear, except for the basics, mask, fins, and snorkel. I did order a couple of BCs, but only one came before the trip. I let Ladema use it. On this trip I had only booked airfare, but knew we could easily get a cheap room downtown. Of course, we stayed at… yes, El Marquéz. Daniel, Don Jorge's son, owner of the El Marquéz, had a small restaurant called Coco's downstairs. I would mail stuff for he and his wife, Terri, when I returned to the states. He and his wife, Terri, were very friendly with us, good people, good food too. The Black Shark Dive Shop was just down the street from El Marquéz. We book four days of diving. I was so excited to show Ladema what the ocean had in store for us. She had already fallen in love with the island, the ocean, the people, the food, with the whole onda of the island. This would be the first of thirteen trips that we would make together.

Our first night there I was seeing things through Ladema's eyes. It was so much fun. We went to dinner at an open-air restaurant right off the square on the malecón. I don't remember what we ate, but I do remember what we drank, one margarita each. I felt fine after finishing my drink, but Ladema was quite inebriated. She only had one drink. We made the short walk back to the hotel. Ladema got quite sick and threw up. She said that she had to stay in the shower. She stayed there most of the night. I went to the store and got her some 7 Up and crackers. I didn't think she would be ready to dive in the morning. Years later we figured out that the margarita probably had tainted alcohol. The following night in our room, Ladema had showered and plugged in her blow-dryer when she got a big shock and blast from the outlet. She was wearing a wide gold band that was blown off her finger. It was sent across the room with great force and there were some small holes burned out in the ring. She was okay.

We went to the Black Shark dive shop the following morning and they drove us to the Caleta Harbor where they kept their boats. Ladema was wearing some nice flip flops and when she went to get into the boat she slipped and fell hard. Her shin bone hit hard on the top side of the back part of the boat. She fell to the floor and had cut her shin. It was bleeding. I didn't think she would be wanting to dive, but no, she sure did dive. On her first and only backroll entry, she proceeded to fall back into the water. She had too much air in her BC and bounced under the boat a bit. I was already under waiting for her. I go quickly up to meet her, and she's got these huge saucer eyes. We surfaced and descended together. Much better. Whew! Averted what could have been the end of her scuba diving career.

Our divemaster with Black Shark on this trip was a kid named José. Ladema took a liking to him. He was funny. He was giving us our briefing and went over some hand signals, like low on air, shark signal with karate chop hand on head, then he made the sign of the cross for "big shark" it made us all laugh.

I had rented a 35 mm camera to take some pictures. I saw a nurse shark in the distance and took off for it to get the shot. It really pissed Ladema that I would leave her there, somewhat bleeding, to get a picture. Oh, I didn't even see it that way. I wasn't leaving her behind, I just needed to get a bit closer that's all. I didn't even get the shot!

On the first dive of our second day, José asked everyone on the boat where we wanted to dive. Someone said Punta Sur! Devils Throat! Okay, no problem. Well, I was excited until I realized that we didn't have lights on us and we were going through a tunnel that started around eighty or ninety feet and comes out just past one hundred and twenty feet. Ladema and I follow the group. It's a small group of four. I thought, *okay, I'll just hold on to the guy's fin that is in front of me and follow.* Well, it's dark and his fin slips through my fingers. Fuck! Okay, we're okay. I know that our tanks are full and that we can always go back. We keep swimming when suddenly, I bump into a wall. Now it's freaking pitch black. Gotta be cool, gotta be cool. I swim to get around and I start to see a little hint of light. Thank you Lord! We swim out very relieved. I'm proud of Ladema cause sometimes she can get a little crazy.

Another divemaster with Black Shark we dove with on other trips was Abraham. He was an older guy. He had also been a chef. He showed us some cool stuff. He was the one who showed me my first seahorse. It was orange and located at the Villablanca Wall reef with its tail hooked onto a long-narrow blue sponge. I was so excited. I got to film it swaying in the current. I could see its individual eyes moving around checking me out. I took some still pics of it and made some enlargements and one poster size. I used to decorate my classrooms with these cool pictures my wife and I have taken. There is so much beauty and wonder under the ocean and every time I dive, I'm excited with anticipation of what I will see or experience on my adventure.

After staying at downtown hotels for our first couple of years, I decided to use RCI to stay in a nicer resort. We stayed at Park Royal (previously Sol Caribe), I've always liked the atmosphere there. We also stayed at the Meliá and at the Reef Club. The Meliá is on the northern end of the island and the Reef Club is at the southern end of the island. The Meliá was closer to town, but the Reef Club was so far south that when we went to San Miguel, it cost us $40 round-trip! We didn't go to town very much on that trip. We had also taken Megan, my freshman stepdaughter, on her first trip to Cozumel. It was the first time that she had taken a trip on a jet. She cried, I thought, "That's weird," but I know it was only because she was just a little nervous not knowing what to expect. The accommodations at the Reef Club were nice with a large beach front. When Ladema and

I decided to go for a swim at the beach, and I do what I always do, check for scorpionfish! Sure enough, I pointed one out to her only a couple of feet away. The fish looks like a stone or rock. A swimmer can easily step on it thinking just that.

We went to Chankanab Park a couple of times on this trip. The first time we went there and hung out at the beach until a supercell storm decides to put a damper on things. It was coming down hard. We stayed under a big palapa, but the rain came in sideways with the wind. We hunkered down around forty-five minutes. I had rented a car; it was a red half-roofed Volkswagon. The floorboard in the backseat had some big holes in it and water was gushing in while driving down the malecón. I had never seen that much rain in Cozumel. There was about a foot of water in the streets and in no time at all it drained out to sea. Cozumel has withstood quite a few hurricanes. As soon as it passes everyone pitches in and begins the cleanup. They take care of business in order to get the tourists to come back. I had gone back after Hurricanes Gilbert and Wilma and all the leaves of the trees on the town plaza had been plucked by the wind. Very sad to see, but I've seen Cozumel come back in a short period of time.

A couple of days later we all returned to Chankanab Park to do a Royal Swim with the dolphins. I bought a waterproof, disposable camera just for the occasion. It was a great experience. We got put into groups of five, us three and a couple of Mexican kids. We got to get pulled by the dolphins by holding onto their dorsal fin. We also got pushed through and up out of the water when pushed from the soles of our feet. We took pictures and bought the video. What a great experience. I did have mixed feelings about it afterwards though. Not knowing how the dolphins were being treated, respectfully, I hope. After talking it over with Ladema, we decided that on our next trip we would have our own cameras. I decided to get a camera to record the wonders. I had gotten a point and shoot Canon SD 630 with a water-proof housing. I gave that to Ladema and I bought a Sony mini-DVD camcorder and an Ikelite housing with two UK light cannons to illuminate underwater. I read a book on underwater videography to get some badly needed tips and I needed to get back to Cozumel to practice!

In June of the following summer, we had our gear and cameras. I would be filming directly onto DVD, and Ladema would take digital stills. At first, I thought that I would just leave the camera on and film non-stop. After viewing the footage, it was like the Blair Witch movie underwater! It was dizzying. So, now I must choose what to shoot and when to pause. On my Ikelite housing I'm looking at a backwards image on a side-mounted mirror. It takes a little getting used to. It seemed that the week just flew by. I felt that I needed to get back to Cozumel asap. So, I did. This time we would be only for a weekend. We took Miranda and Megan, and my cousin, Jon, and his wife, Michelle, would also go. We flew out of San Antonio. While waiting at the airport we had breakfast at McDonald's and Jon was sitting across from me. I had some food in my mouth and proceeded to wash it down with some coffee, when suddenly, I choke and spray my cousin's face with what was in my mouth. He took it well and I apologized. We get to Cozumel without lodging reservations. We walked to Casa Mexicana, but there was no vacancy. We ended up staying at El Marquéz for a night, but we all wanted a swimming pool. We ended up at El Mesón, on the plaza. They had a nice big pool. I never knew they had one. Jon and Michelle joined us on the boat for some snorkeling. Jon cannot swim and had to use one of those orange life-vests. He had a strap that went across his back. He got so sunburned that to this day he still has the sunburn where the strap went across his back. Later we rented a van and drove around the island and made several stops ending at Mescalitos with the girls dancing on the bar. We were the only ones there. We stayed a little while, taking pictures. The waiter took a group pic of us all. Nothing like a cold Dos XX and ceviche!

The diving was great. Finally, on video, sharks! We saw sharks on every dive. We had seen them before but, now we had them on video and still pics. What a fun weekend! On Saturday night we went out and had dinner to celebrate Jon's birthday and later hung out at the plaza. They always have music out on the plaza where all the locals come out and of course, visitors are welcome. While waiting for our meal, there was this elderly gentleman out in front playing the marimba. So, Jon goes and asks him if he can play it and the man was cool and said "No problem." It was so funny watching him play. Pretty good actually, I love that sound.

Ladema and I enjoyed diving with Black Shark Dive Shop. Everyone was very nice, and the price was right. The price of diving has gone up quite a bit since my first trip. I believe they charged $65 U.S. Other dive shops are charging much more. Captain Javier was one cool dude. Since they took out no more than eight on a trip, this is what we prefer. You build relationships and trust. When we would arrive, they would ask me if I could drive their vehicle out to La Caleta harbor. No problem. Captain Javier asked me if I knew what Carmex was, I said yes, and he asked if I could pick some up for him. Again, no problem. He always wore a cool cap with an embroidered blue and yellow splendid toadfish. I asked him how much he would take for it. He said $10. Ten it is. I still have the cap, it's my favorite. It was misplaced for a couple of years, but eventually it was found. The cap is special because a toadfish let me pet it. No shit. As I was coming over a small overhang of coral there lay a toadfish with only its head sticking out. I got close and held my camera my left hand and with my right I lightly rubbed its head with my index finger. It came completely out of its cubby, a beautiful fish. It backed up and went back in. So, I rubbed its head again, and again it came out and returned. I did this about eight times. Luckily, Ladema got a still pic out of it. I didn't video it since I wanted to interact with the fish. Another time Abraham had found a big turtle nearby and had it come our way. I was filming it then it came right up on me and turned around. When it did this, I grabbed it on the shell behind its head to get a little ride. While on the ride, the record button remained on, but did not get anything on video other than when it came toward me. I know I should not have done that. I always try to be respectful to all sea life. I'm so glad I started documenting my dives with video and still pictures. I think I could make ends meet by doing underwater videography and photography. What a cool job to have. So, after I retire from teaching, I'll be moving down to Cozumel to live and work. I guess I could also teach English if I must, but I would rather just dive.

One summer we would spend two weeks at Park Royal just diving and chilling. We did do an excursion to Chichén Itzá. It was the summer it got named one of the "New Wonders of the World."I was dreading going there since it's so hot on the peninsula in the summertime. Luckily, for us it was overcast! Upon entering we see the vendors lined up. They were lined up on all the trails leading to the different temples and such. One of the women asked if we wanted to buy a couple of rain ponchos. I laughed and said, "no gracias." She just smiled probably knowing that we would be back shortly. Sure enough, the sky opened. We hurried back to her to get a couple of ponchos. Well, the already too expensive ponchos became a necessity, and I gave her twenty dollars for the cheapest, flimsiest plastic ponchos that I have ever purchased. There was not much cover anywhere, except a huge tree. Tree? Rainstorm? I know you shouldn't, but we did. We went over with everyone else to seek shelter. I had my camcorder and didn't want it to get wet and kept it underneath my shirt. Our other camera was in its housing, so we didn't have to worry about that one. We waited for around fifteen minutes for it to let up enough to continue. We did check out the observatory, but we could not go up into it. That's pretty much the rule these days. We couldn't go up El Castillo either, nor the Temple of the Warriors. I wanted to see the Chac Mool figure. There's a replica in the Park Royal lobby downstairs with the statue up above. It's called the Chac Mool Bar. Back at Chichén, we walked around and took a bunch of pictures. We walked around the Ball Court. The walls are very tall and high, which is how the Post-Classic Maya made them. The Classic Maya, like of Palenque created much lower and smaller ball courts. The bas-reliefs all along the wall are quite impressive and can be seen very clearly. We did not get to check out the Great Cenote. There were all these tourists who had come from the Cruise Ships because they all had the same-colored rain ponchos, different colors for the various groups.

After leaving we did get to go and check out this one cool cenote, just outside of the ruins. There was like a park with a big palapa where we just chilled for a while. We had a good view of people jumping and diving into it. They would then climb out using some wooden ladders to climb back up. Normally I would have eagerly jumped on in, but I was a little chilled and damp from the rain earlier. Next time. Famous last words. Haven't been back since.

On the route back we made another stop. We pulled into the small town of Valladolid. It was so, so humid. It was stifling. We walked around the plaza and went into the cathedral and took some photos. The heavens open again and it begins to pour hard. We wait it out for about thirty minutes or so before we left for Playa del Carmen where we would catch the ferry back to Cozumel. The driver very meticulously put on his racing gloves before we set out. He was freaking hauling ass on the highway, hydroplaning, and scaring the shit out of us all!

On a previous trip, Ladema and I went to Tulum. It was also a cloudy and rainy day. They no longer allowed people to go up the main pyramid, El Castillo. The ruins are small, and it does not take too much time to get through the site. We did get some excellent pictures. The view of the Caribbean and the pyramids are just spectacular! Just outside of the ruins, on the way to where we would meet our colectivo, I heard some kind of flute music, and it was a bunch of "voladores" sitting on their pole. I guess they were doing their ritual ceremony before coming down by hanging by a line on one foot. They swing down to the ground spinning around. Pretty cool.

In the 80s the ferries were mostly all open air with an upper and lower deck. Nowadays, there can be entertainment like bands or musicians playing for tips. Most all are now air-conditioned.

On one of our trips, we flew out of Corpus Christi on a connecting flight to Houston. Our 9:00 AM. flight was delayed because of bad weather. When we finally took off it was late enough to make us miss our flight out of Houston to Cozumel. Ladema was so stressed out, but what are you going to do? We waited and waited and soon there would be no more flights to Cozumel! That was a very long afternoon at the airport. We ended up taking the last flight to Cancún arriving around 10:00 P.M. We arrive and go to retrieve our luggage, but it did not make it. We waste around an hour there. We then took a taxi to Playa del Carmen for $80 to try and catch the last ferry to Cozumel at 11:00 P.M. We get there too late. The taxi driver offers to take us to a hotel and he drops us off. We stay there the night. We have no clean clothes to change into, well, at least we can shower. We took the ferry early the next morning and check in the Park Royal, but we must go to the airport to get our bags. We go into the Customs Office to get our bags and there is this drug dog there. He doesn't smell the weed that I have in my pocket which I had forgotten that I had. Shit!

Well, Ladema and I dive with Black Shark again and for the last time in the summer of 2007. They were having trouble staying in business. One time we had to change boats to get back, motor problems.

One of my favorite shallow dives was the shipwreck Felipe, as it's called. The ship name was Xico… something. We had dove it before, but this time there was a huge bait ball. It made for good pics and video! They were sardines that were in and around the ship. There was a barracuda up above picking them out and a grouper near the bottom doing the same. We swam through it several times. The fish were right up on the camera lens. It really was spectacular!

On a dive during my descent, I felt my regulator tugging a bit. As I look down, I can see my tank hanging between my legs. I had to drop my camera rig and as I started to unbuckle my BC, Abraham was right there to help me out. Ladema had seen what was going on and signaled Abraham to help me as she was further away from me. On our way back to the Caleta harbor I started to get that seasick feeling. I thought, no way. When I knew that it was inevitable, I took off my cap and put my sunglasses in there and handed them to Ladema. I then leaned over the side of the boat while it's hauling ass to get back. I accidently sprayed a woman from Spain. She screamed at me. "Lo siento," I said. I love México!

In the summer of 2008, we returned in June to dive with Freddy, owner of Mestizo Divers. Freddy used to work with Aqua Safari for many years. He's an instructor and very professional. Everything by the book, safety and no smoking. Dang, I was used to smoking a couple of doobies on our surface intervals on some deserted beach when diving with Black Shark. No matter. Mestizo Divers has a real nice boat and Freddy is very knowledgeable and I enjoy picking his brain. It was nice to get picked up at the Park Royal pier, for

$2.00 U.S. per person! It's just another way to make a buck. All the turistas have money, ¿no? No. We always had some fresh fruit on our surface intervals. Most of the time, it was just Ladema and me diving. I like to dive deep and so I asked Freddy, and luckily enough, he likes to dive deep too. Ladema had never gone that deep before, 150 feet. Got to have good breathing so that you don't suck up all your air too quickly. It feels very calm to me diving that deep. No one can hear you scream.

We visited Cozumel again during the Thanksgiving week. I was already at the Corpus Christi airport when I called in sick. You see as a public school teacher we're not supposed to take personal days right before a holiday. My flight was leaving at 7:00 A.M. for Houston. From there our flight left at 9:00 A.M. for Cozumel. Once again, I made reservations to dive with Freddy at Mestizo Divers. The weather was a little cooler especially being in the swimming pools at Park Royal, but the ocean felt warm. On this trip I spotted my first lionfish, an invasive species from the Pacific. This is bad news for all the little coral fish. It has a voracious appetite and does not have too many predators. Freddy said that some fishermen had found them eaten by groupers. I had mentioned to Freddy that we were planning on going to Palau the following summer and he offered to get Ladema certified as an advanced diver so that she would be able to do some of the more adventurous dives there. That was one vacation where Ladema had to study, read, and do homework. It worked out very well, he only charged her $100!

We dove with Freddy again the following Thanksgiving of 2009. This time my goal was to dive Barracuda Reef on the northern part of the island. I had not dived that part of the island before. I think I dove pretty much all the reefs on the southern end. All great reefs too, but Barracuda is more pristine since there is much less diving. It all depends on the currents. The current is already quite strong making Cozumel mostly drift diving. The best he could do was Punta Raya Reef. It is also on the north end by Barracuda Reef. Freddy said the current was way too strong to dive Barracuda. There was one other diver with us on that trip. I remember Freddy saying, "Okay we need to make a quick descent to the reef to get some protection from the current. If you get swept up by the current start swimming toward the island because the next stop is Cuba!" That really got my attention, but we were all able to get to the reef with no problem. Once there I'm filming and there are all these lionfish up underneath an overhang of reef. These are full grown. I think I heard that the female could lay three hundred thousand eggs each time. Freddy had a little Hawaiian sling. He would spear the lionfish then feed it to sea anemones or triggerfish or even moray eels. I got a bunch of it on video. On our second dive still on the north, I'm not sure what reef it was but we drifted probably about three miles! We were hauling ass and there were so many spotted moray eels everywhere! I had to be careful every time I stopped to film so as not to be bitten by the morays. "What's that thing in the reef with the big shiny teeth... it's a moray." That last sentence is best sung. Before the dive I noticed that the guy had on some Scuba Pro Sea Wing fins. He gladly switched with me. I was wearing split fins. I felt bad for him a bit. He had trouble staying down fifteen feet for his safety stop at the end of the dive. This would be the last time diving with Mestizo Divers. I tried to book other times but he was already booked. They had the coolest t-shirts. On the back was an outline of an ancient Maya blowing out a breath of air. Very cool. I bought several.

For the summer of 2010 we did go diving in Palau. It was fantastic, but that's another chapter. My father had a stroke later that summer and passed on October 1. It was a rough period. We decided to return to Cozumel for the Thanksgiving week. I planned to dive with Dive with Martin. They were located within walking distance from the resort at the International Pier, where all the cruise ships come to dock. I paid for five days of diving for two people. On this trip we left all our gear except mask, fins, snorkel, and computer. Only brought our small point and shoot cameras. It's beginning to be a big chore going through airports with all our scuba gear and camera gear. I've missed connecting flights because the dumbass TSA agents must double scan and check my cameras, lights, etc., even after I explain to them what the items are. On this trip we only dove two of the days. We both were not feeling well, and we went back to the Dive with Martin dive shop and asked them for the remaining dives to be vouchered for future diving. No problem. I kept the vouchers and sure enough the following summer they honored them.

This would have been the summer of 2011. We had originally planned to travel to Egypt for two weeks. One week at the pyramids and ruins and the other week diving in the southern part of the Red Sea out of Marsa Alam. Well needless to say, war broke out and there were travel warnings to Egypt. Okay change of plans. We'll go back to Cozumel, one of my favorite places in the world. We decided that it was time to swim with the Whale Sharks of Holbox, México. We did and it was so awesome. We took off from the Cozumel airport from the private plane area. We chartered a small plane to fly us over the Yucatán to the Isleta de Holbox on the northern end of the peninsula. The pilot was a very cool dude. He offered Ladema to fly the plane since she was seated up front. She politely refused. I was in the back seat filming video the whole way. We landed on a sandy runway near the edge of town. It is a very ecologically conscious community. Only golf carts can be used, no gasoline engines allowed. I had invited my students to come swim with the whale sharks, they just had to meet me at the pier. They would be my guests, no one showed up of course. But I did invite them all.

We got on the boat, and it was Ladema and me, and the captain and his swimmer. Only one person is allowed to swim at a time alongside the whale shark. The swimmer is also out there for safety reasons. I was to be the first to jump in. I had a shorty wetsuit, but I figured the water was going to be quite warm and soupy. To my astonishment, it was freezing cold. The shock made me gasp for air and I ended up swallowing a mouthful of plankton laced Gulf water. It was not the least bit salty. It tasted like brown fresh water. I took some video and got some awesome footage that I'm proud of. We took several turns swimming with the largest fish species in the world, hello! Afterwards, we hand fished for some snapper and they made us some ceviche for lunch right there on the boat. It does not get any fresher than that! They asked if we wanted to snorkel a bit, but we said, no not really, we're divers. We were ready to get on back. We met up with the pilot and headed back to Cozumel. On the way I sat up front. When he asked me if I wanted to fly the plane, I jumped at the chance. I flew it almost all the way back from Holbox. Just as we were crossing the channel coming into Cozumel, he then took over the controls. How exciting that was I have to say.

The following summer of 2012 we had made plans to return to Cozumel in June. Our plans were changed due to the unforeseen circumstances that we now were facing. We took in our two granddaughters ages one and two when their parents split up. No brainer. Ladema quit her job to raise the two girls. We could not leave them with strangers in a daycare. No one was going to watch out for them better than us. I canceled our trip in June and re-scheduled it for early August. It gave us a little time to think about what to do. We decided on taking Holly the two-and-a-half-year-old, and Audrey would stay with my mother and Carlos, her husband in Houston. At the time of our departure, there was a hurricane heading straight for Cozumel. I told Ladema that it would turn and go north. The plane from Houston to Cozumel was nearly empty! I had never seen an airplane so empty going to Cozumel. Only the hardcores were on board of which I consider myself a part. Well, indeed the hurricane did turn north and missed Cozumel.

Holly also loved the water like us. Once put in her little inner tube and she was happy. She's been in a pool from when she was a baby. She'll be a diver one day too. Well, we get to the resort, and I go back to the Dive with Martin dive shop. I show them my voucher and like the last time they honored it. This was now the summer of 2012. I had first made the reservations with them in 2010. I still had three days of diving for two people. Ladema was not going to go dive since she had to take care of Holly. So, I would go dive without my partner. All the time I was diving I was missing them so much that it just wasn't fun. For me, diving is about sharing the experience. Apparently, the diving was great. It was about two years later that I saw the footage from that day. There big green morays, spotted morays, spotted eagle ray, seahorse, the usual angelfish, and triggerfish. They were great dives, but my head didn't really register. I asked them if they could reimburse me for the remainder of my dives and they gladly did, just over two hundred and fifty dollars! Yeah! Let's have some fun my treat!!!

I spent the rest of my time with the two girls. We had fun in the pool, in the dinner hall, at the beach, everywhere. I was seeing my island once again through new eyes. It was damn refreshing. I couldn't think of the last time I had so much fun. Holly was a hit. She got all kinds of compliments and attention. She's always been a good traveler too. We decided to go and check out the San Gervasio ruins. The last time Ladema and I went, we forgot mosquito repellent. Our only recourse was to use suntan oil. Ladema said that there was a cloud of mosquitos constantly following me. I stayed a couple of steps ahead. Well, we remembered the repellent this time. We saw iguanas and took pictures. I remember seeing an episode of "I Shouldn't Be Alive," and it was about a young guy who got lost when he went off the trail. He wandered for days. On the TV they showed what I believed to be a Polynesian Island with sharp peaks. Not Cozumel. I asked the car attendant about that, and he laughed. I think Holly's favorite part was when we went into the gift shop when she spotted a "Dora the Explorer" t-shirt. We all missed Audrey who was back in Houston. From now on we all travel together, where we go the girls go. This would be our last trip until 2016, my last visit to my island.

During the spring of 2016 I took a new teaching position in a small Central Texas school district. I taught junior high there from '95-'99. I had been trying to get back to central Texas for a few years now. I completed the semester, ¡Gracias a Dios! It was my hardest yet. I needed to get away. I was so worried that we wouldn't be able to travel for lack of funds. We eventually got enough money together for the trip. My mother, Clorinda, and Carlos would be traveling with us. They love the girls. They were now five and six. Holly was two and a half when she last went with us. We left out of Houston and arrived in no time. The girls did well on the plane, they thought that it was fun. I think Audrey fell asleep during the flight. This would be the first time ever that I came to Cozumel without any dive plans.

At the airport we went through the usual gauntlet of time-share salespeople to get to the exit. I had rented a car online, or so I thought, and Carlos and I proceeded to the car rental place by the airport. We had to wait, and it was taking longer than I would have liked. Long story short, we walked back to meet up with the girls. They were hot, tired, and hungry and ready to get settled in at the condo. We took the airport taxi to Park Royal. Once there, there was a little problem for us checking in. They had entered our information to the wrong place. Luckily, Ladema had the confirmation number and just had a little wait. Our rooms were on separate floors. We get somewhat settled in our rooms before going to grab a bite to eat.

The following day we went to meet with the time-share people and get upgraded in our lodging. We stayed in the corner Ambassador Suite with the huge balcony with the canopy bed. Nice! Our normal schedule was to eat breakfast then go to the beach for a while. Alternating between the beach and pools. One morning I saved a couple of sausage links to feed the fish in the lagoon. The fish usually keep their distance, but if you have food, that's another story. Well, I start feeding them bits of sausage and the frenzy begins. I get swarmed and Audrey is nearby and gets bitten by a fish and she stomps out of the water mad as hell and not going back in. I finish giving the fish my last bit of sausage, but they want more. One fish took my whole finger into its mouth thinking that it was a sausage. It may have looked like one, but I sure did feel the teeth cutting into me as I pulled it out.

All these years coming to Cozumel, diving has mostly consumed my time. One thing I had never done was go on a Tequila Tour. There were a couple of places in town. There was a place just a little way from the resort and another near the edge of the northern part of town. We went there since we missed the closer one. The person leading tour was a cool guy with the gift of gab. We tried all these samples and they were all very tasty. We got educated on how they go about making the tequila. We ended up buying a bottle of "Regalo de Dios" tequila. No salt or lemon needed, really. It was that smooth.

Something else that I've always seen but never done was the Pirate Ship Dinner Cruise. We were all able to do this. We board the ship there at the ferry terminal. We all took a bunch of pictures there while waiting to board the ship. We finally board and head out. They served lobster, steak, and chicken. The drinks were free, but I probably only had a couple. Carlos, on the other hand, was putting them away! He was taking shots and my mother was slowly starting to get pissed. He was having fun doing push-ups in front of everyone with a girl on his back! I know he was hurting afterwards. Holly was seasick. Not feeling good at all. So sorry mijita.

This being my first time not diving in Cozumel, gave me more time to spend with the girls and my family. I did try snorkeling out of the lagoon at Park Royal, but it was way too bright for my eyes. The glare is too much for me and only made my eyes water. I was disappointed somewhat, but no matter I was in Cozumel! There were other things to see and do. Like, for example, one afternoon we were heading back to our room when we saw a couple guys with an iguana and a camera and we arranged for the girls to have a photo shoot with the iguana. It was fun for them and the iguana, I think, enjoyed it too.

Behind the main building at the resort is an amphitheater. Every night, or most nights, they have some type of cultural show for all the guests. The seating is on cement which is hard on the butt if you sit for too long. We really enjoyed the Mayan Show. They did all these dances and ceremonies and were "dressed to kill." Their costumes were magnificent and looked very authentic. I mean some of them looked like really bad dudes. It was so cool, and the dancers were all so cool too. I wanted Holly to stand with them for a picture after the show. They posed for pictures for everyone. Audrey was tired and had gone back with someone to the room. We waited our turn and finally got our chance for a couple of pics. She looked so innocent amid all these warriors.

PART THREE:
Beyond

21. JAMAICA, LAZY, BUT LIVELY

By the summer of '85, I had been to Cozumel for New Year's and got my Divemaster certification. I kind of wanted to dive somewhere new. I investigated going to Jamaica. I paid the RCI fee and decided that we would fly into Montego Bay and get land transportation to Runaway Bay. Montego Bay was on the northwestern coast and Runaway Bay was about at the center of the island, also on the northern coast. We flew out of Houston and left our car at a "park and go" place near the airport. We landed at Montego Bay and the airport does not have a jetway, so everyone must get off of the plane using the stairs to the tarmac. I could feel the humidity was quite high as my hands started to sweat. Once on the tarmac we all were walking to the gate, when this guy walks up to me and my brother and asks us if we wanted to buy some ganja. I told him, "Hey, this is my mother," and point to her. We kept walking. That guy was probably working with the cops on commission for every tourist that gets busted. Marijuana is illegal in Jamaica! Many people automatically think that it is legal. We change some money for some Jamaican dollars. Their $1.00 bill is very colorful and pretty. I gave some as souvenirs. We finally made our way out of the airport and were supposed to have our travel arrangements already made. Outside there were several tour buses. We were anxious to get on our bus, as there were quite a few people and buses. In our haste, we all got on a bus, and I knew it wasn't the right one. We all got off before it took off. We were going to have to pay. At last, our bus arrived, a bit late, but oh well, we were on the right bus. That guy on the tarmac was still trying to get Adrian to buy some weed. He kept badgering him through the window!

I remember going through the outskirts of Montego Bay. Lots of poor people. I could tell that there weren't very many tourists around. We traveled on the coastal highway. It was scenic. I remember seeing an old bauxite plant. All the buildings were rusted. Soon enough we arrive at our resort. We would be staying at Club Caribbean in Runaway Bay. Our room was an air-conditioned cabaña. It was on the beach. Our cabaña had a loft with two twin beds and looked really cool. It also had a kitchen, living area, bathroom, and bedroom. It was sort of an octagon-shape. There was a meet and greet and the house band played some excellent music. A guy was playing the cajón. It sounded so rich. We made our way over to the dive shop called Sun Divers. We made our reservations to dive three or four days. I did ask Maurice, the bellhop, if he knew where we could "score" some smoke. He went and got us some right-a-way. It was bunk weed. Not too good at all.

The following morning, I met Ricky. He was the divemaster that we dove with. "Ey Mon!" You can usually find some stuff by asking a taxi driver or divemaster. I told him that we had scored some the night before, but that it was no bueno. I asked him if he could get us something of better quality. "No problem, mon." I asked him if it was good, and he said "boom." He then said, "We have to go get a pear!" I'm thinking, *did he just say "pear?"* Yep. He kept saying that we had to try a pear. So, we walk just outside the resort and walk a little way down the road to a fruit and vegetable stand. He told me to ask the woman for a pear, which I did. She then gave me something that sort of looked familiar. It was mostly firm, but I stuck my finger in it. I had to hold it with two hands. It was a huge avocado! It was creamy and tasty.

The following morning, we head out to the dive shop. The water isn't so blue as it is in Cozumel. It is a little greener, blue greenish.

On our first dive my brother Adrian's mask was leaking and he was having some trouble getting down. After the dive he switched out his mask. I had not seen a shark yet, but at Silver Spray Reef, there was an overhang of coral, more like a small cave. Ricky pointed, I looked and saw a wall of small yellow fish. I signaled with open hands, "What up?" He pointed again, this time I saw an eight- or nine-foot nurse shark laying behind the wall of fish. It was huge. My brother Adrian just showed up behind me. I point at it like Ricky did. He only sees the wall of yellow fish. I point, like "over the hill," he gets closer and closer. Then suddenly, the shark comes into focus. He's right up on it almost. He makes the shark sign and gestures to me, "Let's get the fuck out of here!" I gestured back, be cool, with my open palms facing down, and moving in a slow up and down motion. I wanted to enjoy the sight for a little while longer. I motioned for Ricky to pet the shark and he quickly signaled no with his finger. Finally, I see my first shark! The thing about diving in Jamaica, is that you don't see big fish like groupers or angelfish, which aren't that big, except for that big ass nurse shark! In Cozumel you are diving in a National Park where everything is "protected." In Jamaica there are fish traps all around. The bigger fish get trapped and divers go spearfishing. Which is what we did a couple of days later.

Ricky did score us some smoke. He was right. It was boom. It had sort of a spicy taste to it. When you would exhale it through your nose it would kind of "numb" it up some. It came rolled up in newspaper, like a little "bombita." It was inexpensive too. We also were able to get some hash oil. It was a little messy. You could coat a cigarette and cover it with a rolling paper and smoke it out in public. I took my little smokeless pipe. You unscrew it and put the stash in there. There's a rubber mouthpiece so that you don't burn your lips. It hit good. Ricky liked it so I gave it to him.

I had ordered a hamburger there at the resort for lunch. It was okay. I did not like the sweet potato fries though. It was $12.00. That's too much. We took a walk and found a little bakery that sold "beef patties." It was bread stuffed with meat. They were only 25 cents each and oh so good! We got a few for everyone. There was a little store next door to the resort where we went to get some provisions. It also had a small restaurant. One evening, we went to eat supper there. We all had the grilled lobster. It was excellent and for only $7.00 each. We washed it down with some ginger beer. It was more like ginger ale. My first beer at Club Caribbean was a Heineken, but I only drank Red Stripe after that. Along with a Craven A cigarette. Life was good. There at the resort was a few gift shops. They had a bunch of wooden stuff, carving, canes, pipes, etc. We had taken some shirts and a carton of Marlboro cigarettes to trade. My mother had gotten her hair braided twice. The first time was split down the middle, but then had them redo it going the front of her head to the back. It did look better, but it looked painful. Adrian had traded one of the guys that worked there one of his Sassoon shirts. Later that night at the talent show there at the resort he came out wearing it singing some song! I did find one of my favorite t-shirts of all time, it was a Ganja University t-shirt. I treasured it for years after. I bought a carving of a couple of heads on iron wood. It definitely feels like it. They were saying that it was what the police use for nightsticks. At the talent show there was this tiny Rasta dude with huge dreads. He was doing a limbo and his name was Little Bull. He cleared the limbo stick at one foot or less! He was only using his big toes to pull his whole body! Never seen anything like it! It was fun watching and being there. We three guys walked some of the girls home who worked there at Club Caribbean. We walked through some dark AF alleys. Adrian came back first, talking and making friends on his way back. I left and it was very dark. I walked fast, but I didn't want to run. My heart did beat a little faster. Javier came back later.

Ricky kept saying that he wanted to make us an authentic Jamaican meal. He said that we would go spearfishing and get some lobster and fish. We did and got some stop-light parrot fish. Javier made a big batch of rice to add to the lobster, parrot fish, ackee, salfish, green bananas, and dumplings. I saw him make the dumpling. He just made the dough into a ball and threw it in the pot, along with a little ketchup, salt, and pepper. I'm thinking, *that's just masa*. Everything was great for me. I didn't know that parrotfish could be so good! I had to put ketchup on the green bananas because they tasted like potatoes. I took a bite of the dumpling, but it tasted just like plain masa. Ricky asked me if I was going to eat it and I told him no. He put it on his fork and munched it like there was no tomorrow! I did tell him to come by tomorrow morning for breakfast and that we were going to flatten out that dumpling and make some taquitos. Good thing mom was there. She made some tortillas. She had to use butter instead of lard which gave it a yellowy-look with a buttery taste. She made some egg and potato taquitos. Ricky knocked on the door around 8:00 A.M., before going diving. I gave him the taco and told him to take a bite. He did and the light shined in his face and he had an "AHhhh" moment. He opened the taco and said, "You put the egg and the potato together?" Yeah, Mon! Breakfast was great. We go diving and I think we dove Canyon. It like these huge "canyons," walls you swim in between. Pretty cool. I remember finding tiny sand dollars and trying to bring them up to the surface, but they were so delicate that they would disintegrate while ascending. I did manage to bring up a light-greenish sea biscuit. I had set it on the Zodiac boat, but Winston, the boat driver, had set a tank on it and broke it into smithereens. Oh well. Whatcha gonna do?

My mom wanted to try parasailing. I would have too but spent all of my oney on diving. This was "old school" parasailing where you are on the beach and must walk with your arms spread out. The boat pulls you while you're walking towards the ocean. Well, my mother starts walking, but tries to "chicken out" at the last minute, but it's too late. She kind of stumbles a bit and the boat takes off and yanks her up quickly. She keeps going higher and higher. Let me add that she's terrified of heights! To land, the boat comes as close to shore as it can, parallel to the beach and while the parasail is descending, you're supposed to pull it down on one side of the chute, lowering it down to the beach. I said a prayer and I told Adrian to get ready to catch her. As she was coming in on her final round, the boat started coming in and slowing down. I could see that she was trying to pull the chute on one side and managed to pull it down enough to get herself on the beach. Adrian and I did manage to keep her from crashing harder than she did. That was brave of her. One day she went on one of our dives. Ricky really took a liking to her, like a mom. Anyway, on our surface interval she *did* try to scuba. She got all the gear on in waist high water, and she went down for a little bit, but came back up. She said she felt too claustrophobic. She wasn't used to having all that gear on. She already feels uncomfortable in the water. Hey, at least she tried.

OLetne day I walked down to the road and asked George, the taxi driver, if he would drive us around the countryside. "No problem, Mon." I think he charged us $20.00, and I gave him a pack of smokes. Javier was in the front seat and Adrian, my mom, and I were in the back. I asked George if we could smoke some ganja in his car. No problem, mon. So, we did. My mom was cool about it. The night before she had gotten so stoned, we all had a good laugh. Driving through the countryside, everything was so green and lush. We would go west and loop around and come eastward to Ocho Rios. We first stopped at Discovery Bay which just down the road from the resort. It was where Columbus was stranded on his fourth voyage to the New World. We took some pictures. There was also a grotto that we had gone to where some slaves had escaped through, getting away from the English. We stopped somewhere in the country to

114

take a leak and some pictures. Everything is so lush and green. On the drive we're going up and down some hills. On the way down, I could hear George "pumping the brakes" to slow down. Javier said, yeah, he was pumping the brakes like crazy. We continue our way to Ocho Rios. George said, "Hey you know that Ocho Rios means Eight Rivers in Spanish?" We all looked at each other and said, "Really?" "Yeah Mon." We go to a restaurant and tell George to order what he wanted. He ordered "curry goat." We all order, I can't remember what I ordered. But I'm looking at George's dish and it looks delicious. I asked him, "Hey George can I try your curry goat?" "No problem, Mon." "It's cabrito!" I yell out. He sure had the best meal of all. I thanked him. After our meal, we went out to check out some crafts markets. Dunn's River Falls was there nearby. At the market, this one guy asks Adrian, "Hey Mon, what's your name?" He says Adrian. The guy starts to carve his name on a bamboo cup and then insists that he buy it! They were quite aggressive when it came to pushing their wares. If someone saw you buy something from someone else, then they would want you to buy something from them as well. I did buy a couple of canes and gave one to my friend Jim and one to my grandmother. I kept the pipe of a naked woman to myself. I still have it. On our way back to Runaway Bay we have a flat tire. We were at St. Ann's Bay. It was a short distance from the resort. We walk down a bit to the beach area and there are some swings. The mosquitos are out too. George gets the tire fixed and we head on back to the resort.

We've had such a good time that it was going to be hard to leave. We became friends with Wickford "Ricky" Williams. That was his full name. He said that he didn't want to see us off because he would cry. He did see us off and cried! Before we left, I did score a quarter ounce of "just what the doctor ordered." I put it in my boot wrapped in foil. What a moron! I don't know what I was thinking! I'm a little paranoid. As we get closer to the security checkpoint at the airport,

Adrian says "Hey man they're making some guy take off his boot! Scared the shit out of me! He was just joking. To make it through Customs I think about "puppy breath and flowers." Seems to work. I did get the weed back home and got to share it with friends. A couple of weeks after we get back home, my mother receives an envelope from Ricky labeled "photos." On the envelope he had written her Texas driver's license number on it, along with her address. The only thing, it wasn't photos, it was a least an ounce of weed! He had pressed it down pretty good. It was such a surprise to her that it scared her a bit, having her information out there for all to see. She and Carlos were friends with someone in their apartment complex that gladly accepted her gift. Lucky guy! I wish she would have given it to me!

22. ALASKA, VISITED AND RE-VISITED

It was August of 2008 and Ladema and I had already spent two weeks in Cozumel making excursions to the Yucatan. Now, it was time for me to show Ladema what I had been talking about. She had always wanted to go up to the Great Land. I lived and taught in Homer during the '99-2000 school year. That's another story.

We flew out of Houston on a direct flight to Anchorage. We arrived around 10:00 P.M. We picked up our rental car there across the street at the airport and checked into a nearby hotel for the night. The best Alaskan vacations should be at least two weeks to a month to see what all there is to do, there's lots! Us poor folk can only afford one week on a teacher's salary at this time. This is our best shot so here goes…

Early the next morning, we have a hearty breakfast there in the downtown area of Anchorage. We walked around a while and go into some Native American craft shops. The streets look so nice with flowerpots with lots of flowers on the lamp posts, I think they were *forget me nots*. Ladema really likes it already. We head on out north to the McKinley Princess Lodge in Denali National Park. It's on the southern end. On our way up, there's a sign to Talkeetna. It's only a few miles and I had always wanted to but never got the chance to go for a visit. So, we take a right and drive on to Talkeetna. They say that it's the closest town in Alaska that looks like the town in the show "Northern Exposure." Loved that show! Ladema says that we went to the lodge first, but I disagree, and anyway, it's my book! So, we get there it looks so Alaskan. We had some good Chinese food there for lunch from a little place there on the town square. Well, it's more like a downtown area. There is some quaint little gift shops that we went into. We were just waiting for a moose to start walking across the street! We would be returning in the next couple of days. We drive to the lodge and as we're making our way through the entrance, we see a mother black bear and her cub crossing the road.

We would be staying at the McKinley Princess Lodge. It took a little while to find the office. It was spread out with units on one end and the main lodge, gifts shops, and restaurants on the other end. The grounds were nice. There were statues of bears, wolves, and eagles. There was quite a few hiking trails and a vegetable garden. In the main lodge there was a great room with a wall of windows with a view of Mt. Denali, when visible. There was also a huge open fireplace and dining room. I had a couple of Snickers caramel macchiato coffees there at the bar. They were so good that I guzzled them in about fifteen minutes.

After checking in, Ladema and I walked on one of the trails. She made sure to buy a little bell that you could tie to your shoe to alert the brown bears that you are around. You *do not* want surprise or spook one, especially if it's a sow with cub. It was drizzling so good thing we took our Texas Longhorn rain ponchos. They are of good quality and soon enough we were getting hot. Ladema rang the hell out of that bell as we were walking. At one point on the trail, we could see a river down below with people doing some white-water rafting. I don't think we would be doing any rafting this time, but we are interested in a flight-seeing tour of Mt. Denali with a walk on Ruth Glacier. We book a tour for the following day.

Later that night we have dinner in the dining hall. We were out on the huge observation deck looking through the telescopes, trying to catch a glimpse of Denali with no luck. There are too many clouds. We go back in, sit down, and order. I'm having the Halibut and Ladema gets the King Crab. My eyes get huge when I see Ladema's entrée. There are all these very large crab legs that are already slit for easy access. All she had to do is dig it out and dunk it in some garlic-butter sauce! I practically inhale my meal so that I can help Ladema with hers. OH MY GOD! This is my best meal ever! I can't believe how good it is, I guess I had forgotten since it's been a while that I've had some. I had to get a picture of her dish and I used my camera. Now, I'm not one to take pictures of food, I just barely got a smart phone, and that's because it was given to me. Thank you, iCanConnect!

The next morning, we board the Princess Bus to Talkeetna for our flight-seeing tour of Denali and glacier walk. We get to the airport and sign in and make our way to our group and plane. I have my camcorder and am filming. I wanted to get the briefing and starting to record. The pilot gets pissed and tells me that I must pay attention, I freaking was! Rather than me being an asshole, I put it down until we got into the plane. I recorded the take-off. It was a long ass plane ride. I already had to pee as it was a little chilly in the plane. There were two other couples besides us and the pilot. We all had headphones and mics with which to communicate with each other. Finally, we get closer to the mountain. The pilot flies around a bit to where the glacier is. I already decide that I was going to pee on it once we landed. The weather reports were that it had snowed the night before and that having fresh snow would make our landing a bit more unstable. He didn't want to take the chance, so we aborted that mission. When we got back to the lodge, I did get refunded some money since I had paid for something and didn't get it. We make our way back and it doesn't seem as long. As soon as we get back to the airport I rush to the restroom, but there's someone in there, fuck! I finally get in, but I had already started to "spot" the front of my pants.

Back at the lodge we have dinner at the 20,308 Restaurant and retire early to our room. It was nice. The water was so cold. I think it was glacier water. It was delicious too. When we left the following morning, I had forgotten a pair of Nikes underneath my bed. Dang, I liked that pair!

We start our drive back south, through the Mat-Su Valley and on through Anchorage. I did stop in Wasilla at a hardware store to get an alligator clip for my roaches. Anyway, we head on down the Turnagain Arms to the Kenai Peninsula and on to Seward. I had wanted to do a Kenai Fjords Tours and check out the Alaskan Sea Life Center on Resurrection Bay. We get to our hotel and check in. We drive around a bit. We found the high school stadium from atop a hill. There was a glacier nearby that we went to check out. We parked by the road and just looked at it from afar. We came there a couple of times for a doobie break. We drove closer to it and parked. We were going to walk up to it, but for some reason we could not or did not.

The next morning, we drove to the harbor where we would board our ship for the Kenai Fjords Tour. It was a very good size ship. We would be having prime rib and lobster for lunch. I remember seeing this one guy, he had a tank top with shorts and sandals. He had to be an Alaskan showing how tough he was. Way more than me I can tell you for sure! I had a jacket and pants, and I was freezing my ass off! I must have gone to the bathroom at least thirty times or more on the five-hour tour, no kidding.

We hit the open ocean and our captain got a message from another captain that they were seeing some orcas in the area. We go in that direction and can see a pod of some. Everyone on the boat rushes up to the front of the boat to get a view. Ladema and I were in the right spot already. We did take some pics. We met a young

German couple who had been traveling around Alaska. He showed me some of his pictures on his camera. Wow! Close-ups of bears! Great shots! I then knew that I had to get a better camera than the point and shoot model I had.

We would go into some bays where the glaciers were, hoping to catch them calving. It would sound like a shotgun blast before it would calve. We only got to see some smaller ones. We waited for a big one, but to no avail. The ship got further into the bay where they got some of the ice floating in the water to make drinks to sell. In some of the other bays were seals and I finally got to see some puffins. They are one of my favorite birds. We got some good pics. It's time to eat and it's okay. The Germans loved it. They couldn't get enough. They kept going back for second helpings. At this point, I've already seen enough and am ready to start heading back.

The morning we left Seward, we had breakfast in a restaurant made from a train caboose. It was so cool. The breakfast was good, I mean how do you mess up breakfast? I'm excited that we would be going to Homer next. We head on out of Seward and make a left turn going down the peninsula to Homer. We stopped at that Russian Orthodox Church with the green tin roof. Alaska is so scenic that there are pull outs all along its highways. From where we were you could see a volcano. I forget which one it is, Iliamna or Redoubt. Ladema got out and went for a closer look. There was no one around. We peeked into the church and left. Driving through Soldotna I pointed out Mt. Redoubt, it's a volcano. I love seeing the Kenai River. I still dream of catching a big king salmon in that pretty turquoise water. We're about an hour and a half from Homer. I start recognizing the land and finally coming over the hill into Homer you see the bay and the mountains. It truly is beautiful! It's jaw-dropping. OMG! I can't believe I finally made it back. I see the Welcome to Homer sign, The Halibut Fishing Capital of the World! Tru dat! I drive through town and on to the Spit, where we would be staying at Land's End Resort. We checked in and drove down East End Road, to where I used to live. It's a few miles just past Fritz Creek. I saw the house I used to live in, and they had put a new roof. It must have caved in with all the snow. It used to have a flat roof when I lived there. I had to shovel it a couple of times for fear of it caving in. We went further down the road. It curves to the right just past McNeil Elementary. There used to be a big trash bin near the literal "end of the road." It's the end of the westernmost road on the connected highway system in North America. Now the pavement had extended for miles and miles. We went down a good way. Further down is where the Kilchers live, the homesteading families on "Alaska: The Last Frontier" show on Discovery. We turn back and head into town. Passing the high school and stadium, I noticed that they were having a football game. Great! We parked there at the high school and walked to the stadium; it was nearby. This stadium has the most scenic view of any stadium that I've ever seen! The bleachers face the bay and the mountains in the background. I had my camcorder and filmed some of the game. I made sure to get the background! I saw that Cam was the Head Coach now. He and I coached the JV and Freshman teams back in 1999. I went down to the field to say hi. I asked him if he remembered me? He said yes. I left quickly so as not to distract him any more than he might have already been. We sit and enjoy the game for a while and especially the view. Ladema was really wowed. I bought a pair of Homer Mariner shorts to help support their program.

After the game we head to the Spit and grab a bite to eat at Glacier Burger. I always liked their food. This time was no different. Not to mention, it has great views. We then check in at North Country Charters. We'll be going halibut fishing tomorrow and make sure everything is in order. We'll have to get a temporary daily fishing license. They tell us that there was a place where we could place an order tonight and pick it up in the morning around 5:00 A.M. before we go fishing. We do that and head on back to the hotel.

Our room is very nice, and we decide to have dinner there at the hotel. I think I had the halibut, again. I had a Red Knaught draft. I believe that it's from a local distillery. We turn in as morning will come very soon.

We get up early AF! We go and pick up our box lunches and head on out to the harbor. We meet Captain Jack, our boat captain. We, along with a family, would be going on the fishing charter. The captain did everything for us like baiting our hooks and gaffing the fish into the boat. We were still in Kachemak Bay when I caught my first halibut in shallow water. It wasn't deep at all. I reeled it in, and it was a keeper, about 35 pounds! I was ready for some more! Ladema caught one too, yeah! I remember her asking Captain Jack, "How do I hold the pole?" He answered, "Anyway you can!" We were using "ugly sticks." It's a short and sturdy pole. I start reeling in my bait to see if it was still on there. You can feel the fish nibbling at the bait. Nope, and I drop it again. This time we're in much deeper water. It's a workout to reel in the bait or naked hook. I catch what feels like a VW and put it up and it's only about a fifteen pounder, fuck! Throw it back! That sucked hard.

I'm a little tired and decide to take a break. Ladema already had her break and was fishing again. I climb up on the higher deck on the roof of the boat and get my camera out. Suddenly, the captain yells out that there are some whales over in the distance. I get my camera ready with anticipation. He said that yesterday they were breaching the surface. As I looked at the water near the boat, I could see tiny krill everywhere. I was hoping that they would come closer, and they did! It was a mother Humpback whale and her calf.

She let a big spray from her blowhole. It had a fishy stink to it. She came right up close to the boat and the captain tells us to hang on to something. He said that they sometimes bump into the boats. You don't want to fall into the water. Ladema asked me if I was getting all the footage, I said, "Yeah, baby." This was so exciting. We had seen some Orcas earlier in the week and now this close-up with the Humpbacks was just amazing. Life is good. We decide that we're going to keep the next fish we catch. We get our two halibut each and head on back to Homer. The captain shows off our catch of the day for pictures and we pose with the fish. They have someone fillet the fish and walk it over across the street for flash-freezing at Coal Point Foods. We're both tired and hungry.

We get back and drive to restaurant just off the Spit and get some buffalo burgers. They were okay, a bit dry, but a buffalo steak would have been much better. We went to some gift shops in Homer. I had to stock up on baseball caps. On our way back to the hotel, we looked around at the shops on the Spit. We went into the Salty Dog and Ladema bought one of their long-sleeve t-shirts. We head on back to our room.

The following morning, we would go and pick up our halibut. They told us the boxes only held up to 50 pounds. I had a few more. He said we could take them or donate them to food kitchens. I donated them not knowing that they would stay frozen all the way back to Texas! Knowing that now, I would have just stuck them in my backpack. They would have been fine and would not have melted.

Making our way of the Spit we pulled over so that Ladema could take some pictures of a bald eagle on a pole. It was just off the road by a nearby house. We got some shots of the eagle and made our way out. What a trip! I love Alaska and now so does Ladema! I had wanted to stop and eat at the Seven Glaciers Restaurant near

Girdwood which is not far from Anchorage, but we didn't get to. We ate Chinese somewhere in Dimond Center. We turned in our car and proceeded to check-in with our flight. Going through the terminal, I felt so proud walking through the airport with my box of halibut!

I saw guys with two or three boxes! That's hardcore! As it turns out, Mt. Redoubt decided to act up and erupt. It bellowed ash into the atmosphere and all flights were delayed. What are you going to do? You know the more you travel the more shit happens! I've had countless times when my luggage didn't make it with me and had to be delivered to my hotel or home by the airline company. Well, our delay was a couple of hours or so. Probably closer to three hours. We went outside of the terminal a few times to stretch our legs and have a smoke. We sat on the grass just outside the terminal. It was a nice evening. We did indeed catch our flight shortly thereafter and soon departed for Houston.

I was really proud walking through the George Bush International Airport in Houston with my box of halibut. I shared the halibut with family and friends. I can't wait to go back for more and take the girls next time!

23. PERU, CUSCO, AND MACHU PICCHU

I have always dreamed of going to the Amazon ever since I was a child. Not too many people like to venture out into a jungle. It is so freaking awesome! Ladema and I planned our trip and left for South America in early June, just in time for the Corpus Christi Festival and Inti Raymi, the Incan New Year. As it turns out, the airline had overbooked. Yes, it happens! So, the airline offered us two $400 travel vouchers. We would have to take a later flight to Miami, then on to Lima. We would be at the Lima airport around 11:00 that night. Well, we do go to Miami and wait a short while on the plane. Other passengers boarded and we were off to Lima. We did get there around midnight. I had a hotel reservation at a nearby hotel, but I didn't really want to leave the airport since our flight was leaving around 5:00 A.M. for Cusco. So, I called the hotel to tell them that I wouldn't be coming. They said they could have someone to pick us up at the airport shortly. I told him thanks, but we'll just stay at the airport. We practically stayed up all night. I wrote a letter to the airline saying that we would be going to Cusco and to please deliver our backpacks there. I slid the note under the door. Everything was shut down. Around 4:00 A.M. some airlines started opening. What really caught my attention was seeing all the airline workers with surgical masks on. Ladema and I looked at each other, *Is there something that we should know about?* We did have to get a yellow fever vaccine since we were going to the Amazon. At the airport, I thought that I had seen my grandmother. She died in 1999. I looked again to see if it was a woman that looked like her, but she was gone! I was getting tired, but it was soon time to finally get on our plane to Cusco. Oh, my new favorite drink is Inka Kola. It's like a cross between crème soda and mountain dew with a dash of bubble gum.

We get to Cusco and there's tons of people waiting for others to come off the plane. Luckily our hotel, Casa Andina, had someone come over and pick us up. They had a sign that read Juventino Morin. I saw it and was relieved to get my ride! On this trip we took regular backpacks. I had a Kielty that works well. However, our backpacks didn't make it to our hotel at the same time as us. We drove through the outskirts of Cusco to near the central part of the city. If you look at it from up high, Cusco looks like a navel. Its name means the "navel of the world." Our hotel is on an incline and is very nice. It was warm and sunny. We were exhausted. They at the hotel, offered us some coca tea. We drank it and it tasted okay, like tea. We checked into our room. The bed was very comfortable with a down comforter! It was so soft. We showered and put some nice robes they had there and fell asleep. We were awakened by a knock on the door. It was our luggage, our backpacks! Yeah! Gave the guy a tip and we were so grateful to get our stuff.

It was still early in the day, and we could feel the effects of the altitude. At the hotel, the guy behind the desk told us that we could get some coca leaves for some quick relief. We walked down the street, literally, to the Central Market. We walked through and I asked someone where I could get the coca and he pointed to a lady. I asked the lady if she could sell me some coca leaves. She filled a good size bag and charged me $1.50. She gave me a chunk of pure cacao. She told me to put it in some leaves and cover it. It helps activate the coca. It's like chewing tobacco, sort of. It just tastes green. You could feel it numbing your lip a little. We walked around and found the place where Anthony Bourdain had some soup. So, we had some noodle and vegetable soup, good and cheap. As I looked around, there didn't seem to be any gringos around, except for Ladema. Afterward, just outside of the market was a church. I think it was the San Pedro Church. There were tourists walking around with their backpacks in front on their chests! They looked like a bunch of morons. I was embarrassed for them. I did read that tourists have had their packs cut from the strap and taken. I truly felt safe and at no time did I feel threatened. We head on towards La Plaza de Armas and La Catedral. Our Spanish II textbook had a picture of the blue door of the Catedral. I decided to pose in front to get my own shot.

It was the beginning of the Corpus Christi Festival. It was hopping! There at the plaza we were just shooting pictures like crazy! There was so much to see and lots going on. You had the school children in their uniforms all together. You had people coming from their villages from all over Peru! It was so colorful. They had their local dress customs. Some of the men wore cool AF gorros. The ones with beads and tassels. So freaking cool. Coming out from inside the Catedral were statues of all these saints. They were carried on the shoulders of the men. They would walk the saints down the steps of the cathedral. You could tell that it was quite heavy. Even the military was present. There were soldiers also participating. We couldn't get enough pictures!

For the trip I bought a Canon Rebel SLR digital camera, very nice. I also bought a zoom lens for it. In addition, I got a Canon Vixia Camcorder, also very nice. Upon reading the owner's manual for the Vixia, it read that it should not be turned on higher than 9000 feet above sea level, due to hard-drive damage. Crap! Cusco is at 11,000 feet! Oh well, at least I could use it at Machu Pichu which was at around 8,000 feet. At least Ladema could use the Rebel while I would use the Canon point and shoot for video. We had dinner and turned in. I had arranged for a tour tomorrow of the sights around Cusco. Our room was on the second floor, and you could see down to the patio where we had supper that night. It was a little cool and the waiter came over and turned on the outdoor lantern heater. It felt so good!

We had breakfast there at the hotel and were picked up by the tour bus. We met our tour guide at the Church of Santo Domingo, or the Templo del Sol, also known as Korikancha. Our guide spoke English to our group. He was a young guy and very knowledgeable. We went in and first saw the courtyard. It was flying the Cusco flag. Earlier the day before a woman came up to me and pinned a Cusco flag on my shirt. It's the Rainbow Flag. We walked around and saw the different stonework. Some of the stone blocks would interlock with each other. He showed us the tiniest of stonework. He said that it was a sign of power. In other words, they could make them stones as big or as small as they wanted. We came out to the front of the temple looking out to the garden. It was a fenced in area with nice grass. Our guide told us that the Incan kings had life-size statues of solid gold in the shapes of llamas, condors, pumas, and other regional animals. When the Conquistadores came and took them to Spain, the soldiers said, "Look, my King!" Charles V answered, "Hmm, melt them and make gold coins." I believe that there are still some pieces in museums. That was pretty cool.

Well, it's time to leave and we all board the bus. I notice this man on our tour. He keeps rubbing the back of his head. I think he's having a headache due to the altitude. I was already chewing on some leaves but had also bought some coca candy. I went over to him and offered him some. He quickly took them and ate some. Later, I noticed that he was doing a little better. At our next stop there was a vendor selling some of that candy and saw that he had bought some. We stop at a place called Laberinto. It was like rock formations where they would sacrifice animals and the blood would run through the labyrinth of carvings on the cave floor. We headed on out to Sacsayhuaman. It was very impressive. The stones were huge and fit together perfectly. Across the field from the fortress were stone formations that were used as slides for the locals just wanting to have some fun. On one end you could see chairs that were being set up for the Inti Raymi celebration which was in a few days. The wind started to pick up and I was only wearing a shirt. I stayed behind a big stone to break the chilly wind. Ladema had a jacket and was fine. We get a bunch of pictures and get back on the bus. At our last stop, Tambomachay, the trail kept going up and further up a hill. We stopped to take some pictures. At the top there was an aqueduct or something that was feeding water through a wall. The guide said that it has flowed continuously since Pre-Columbian times. One guy in our group asked, "Hey, can you drink the water?" The guide answered, "Yes, but you might have diarrhea for life!" We all laughed. In the meantime, I scoped out this woman who is selling alpaca woolen sweaters and ponchos. I ask the lady how much for the poncho. She said $65. Okay then. I really didn't care how much it was going to cost. I had been freezing my ass off there after sundown. After, our tour we went to a shop above Cusco to get some tea and enjoy the view of Cusco. It was incredible! You could see the whole city. All the lights, there was a stadium too. What a view! The store we were in had all these woolen products, but I was tired already and was ready to turn in as we would be heading to Machu Picchu by train early the next morning.

The following morning, I picked up the train tickets at our hotel desk. We took a taxi to the train station and were there at 6:00 A.M. It was cold and damn early. I asked the taxi driver if he could meet us back here in a couple of days at 4:00 P.M. No problema. So, Ladema and I board the train and it had windows on the ceiling so that you could see the mountains all around. It was covered in ice! We only had a soda on the train. Our travel companions who were sitting across from us were two girls of high school age. One was from Bolivia and the other one was from Colombia. I asked them if they had any coca leaves. They said no, so I gave them some. I still had a lot. It's customary to share them. I think it took close to three hours to get to Aguascalientes or Machu Picchu Town. On the way we make a stop at Ollantaytambo. We bought a very cool looking backpack from a woman through our train window. We didn't want to get off the train since it was not going to be there for very long. At last, we make it to Aguascalientes. We walked from the train station to our hotel. Shit, there were mountains all around us! We find our hotel and check in. On our way from the hotel to town there was this one little parrot out in front of a house. He had a little bucket that said "tips." We had to stop and give him some $$. There were some coins on the ground that didn't make it into the bucket. I picked them up and put them in. He would take it in his beak and drop it into the bucket, or least try to. I got some good video! We walked around town. I was checking out my new video camera. The color is excellent in high definition. It was so tiring walking around. Ladema and I had dinner there in a restaurant on the square. We were outside and the colors of the surrounding jungle was so freaking green! I took some video of the statue of Pachacutec. He was the king who did a lot of building. Later that night, Ladema and I wanted to go and checkout the hot baths. There's supposed to be these hot springs. We walk up an inkling hill for quite a long way before we finally find the place. There are these different pools of warm water. There was only one pool that shot out hot water. We stayed there for a short while, somewhat disappointed. We head back down and on our way, we stop at a little café down the street. A gentlemen came by selling his crafts. He had the gorros that I was looking for. Earlier in the day Ladema and I went to the crafts market. They tried to sell her one for $120 and when I went to the same person he told me $60! Big difference, ¿no? We bought some other stuff from him. He charged me only $20 for the gorro. It was beautiful. It took a lot of work. I regret not buying three. We also saw some very cool artwork in a gallery down the road. There were some excellent pieces. We head on back to get some rest. Tomorrow was going to be a big day and I couldn't wait! Going to Machu Picchu finally!

Our hotel was decent, we left Ladema's backpack there and only took mine with some of her stuff. We got a ticket for the bus going up to the citadel. The bus takes the switch-back road up to the top of the mountain. It's amazing that the drivers can get two buses on the road at the same time, one going and one coming. We get to the top and it parks in front of the Machu Picchu Sanctuary Lodge, where we would be spending the night. It was quite expensive, $975 for one night! I figured that it was only three days of work and this was a trip of a lifetime! So there! We couldn't check-in quite then as it was a little early. We left our stuff and went to the ruins of Machu Picchu. We walk on the sidewalk and look at the big map they have there at the entrance. I'm looking at it and looking around. I walk over to where the guides are and hire a woman for $35. We start entering and she asks, "Do you want the regular tour or the easy one for older people?" No, we want the regular tour. Okay, so we start heading up and up climbing to the highest part of the ruins. There was a guard house up there. Got to take some iconic pics of Huayna Picchu in the background. So, freaking cool! We walked all around and started making our way back down. What a place. I went up to the Intihuatana, the Sun Dial, there's a rope around the big stone so you can't get too close. A woman was leaning over and said, "I can feel the vibrations." After she left, I went over, but nope. I couldn't feel anything. As lunch time was approaching, we made our way back to the hotel. We finally checked in and went in to have lunch. There was a big lunchroom with an Andean music band. I went up and posed for a picture with them. The lunch was very good. I got to try all these different types of ceviche. Ceviche is the national dish of Peru. Everything was so good. We went back to our rooms to rest up a bit and get some more coca leaves!

It was early afternoon when we decided to go back to the ruins. We walked in and there was practically no one there, except for the llamas. We had the place pretty much all to ourselves! How awesome is that! We walked all over the place. Got to get some video of Ladema petting one of the llamas. We also got some video of two chinchilas. They called them "conejos." They sort of look like a rabbit, but their tail was curly. We saw some of the kitchen staff posing for some pictures that were going to be put on a billboard somewhere in Cusco. They all posed for us. I videoed a bus coming up the switch-back road. It was muddy and sliding all over the place. My video camera has some good zoom on it. After we get our fill of the place and are tired, we decide to head back to get some supper. We walked around the grounds and saw that they had all these different types of orchids! It was so cool. We even saw some in the ruins as well.

Our plan was to wake up very early the following morning so that we could get on the list to climb Huayna Picchu. We were to be up by 5:00 A.M. We both overslept and it was 6:00 A.M. and a long line had already started forming to sign up to climb Huayna. Two groups are allowed at a time. The first group of 200 can go from 7:00 A.M. to 10:00 A.M. The next group was from 11:00 A.M. to 1:00 P.M. It was a no brainer for us to go at 7:00 A.M. since it's cooler. We get to the guard house and have to write down all our information, like next of kin. Seriously! People have had fatal accidents before, and they have to know where to ship the body. So, we put down all our information and get on the trail. As we're walking you could smell urine along the way. Ooh it stunk! We start climbing and climbing. While we're taking a break there's this one older couple maybe in the 70s, had just passed us up with a bounce in their step! Oh, hell no! Ladema and I kept on. At another rest spot, I'm huffing and puffing bent over with my hands resting on my knees. Ladema feels in her pocket and realizes that she hadn't given me my meds, so she gives me my blood pressure medicine! I quickly took it. We didn't even have enough time for a cup of coffee! All I had was a small bottle of water for both of us, some trail mix, and coca leaves. We were all right and made it to the top! It took us around an hour. We took pictures of Machu Picchu from up there. It looked tiny. Got some great video too. You could see the snowcapped Andes in the distance. It was an incredible feeling. I shared my trail-mix with another Spanish teacher and his family we had just met at the top of the mountain. I shot video with the small camera on the way back down. Just as dangerous as going up if not more, according to some. We finally made it down! We were so tired! We walked to the hotel and checked out. We took the bus back down the mountain and had to go back to the other hotel in Aguascalientes where we had left Ladema's backpack. First, we go to a little restaurant by the railroad tracks. I had a couple of glasses of tea. I was so freaking tired! As I was having a smoke, the waiter asked me what kind of cigarettes was I smoking. I had about five or six American Spirits left and gave them to him. He said that he collects cigarette packs. After, we go to the hotel to retrieve our backpacks and they were so freaking heavy. I asked the hotel guy if he could take them to the train station for me. No problema. He grabbed them both and darted out in front of us. He was hauling ass! People who live there walk like it's no big deal. When we finally catch him at the station, I give him a $20 and he doesn't want to take it. I tell him, please please you helped us out big time in my book! He reluctantly takes it. We board and head on back to Cusco. We're seated with a couple from Scotland. They kept us quite entertained. They told of their travels to Africa, India, and Sri Lanka and places like that. They were so funny. And I was wearing my Macallan cap, it's a brand of scotch and I don't even drink scotch. It was such a fun conversation. When we get back to the train station in Cusco, our taxi guy is there waiting. Fuck yeah! I say that we were glad to see him. You know, many people visit Machu Picchu. They come in on the train and stay for a few hours and head on back to Cusco. I'm glad that we took two whole days there. It was a great time with many memories. We get back to the Casa Andina Hotel where we would stay the night. We would be flying out to Puerto Maldonado and on to the Tambopata Reserve in the Amazon.

24. Peru, Puerto Maldonado and the Amazon

We left a couple of our bags at the Casa Andina Hotel and would be back to get them when we returned from the jungle. We would be staying at the San Blas Boutique Hotel in the San Blas neighborhood when we would return to Cusco. We took a taxi to the airport and headed to Puerto Maldonado. It was a short flight, not even an hour. I decided on Puerto Maldonado, rather than Iquitos since it had less of a human print. You can only enter the jungle with a licensed guide. We would be going to the southern part of the Amazon via Puerto Maldonado. I decided that we would go with the Wasai Lodge. When we arrived at Puerto Maldonado, the airport was like a free-for-all. We start walking out of the terminal and everyone wants us to go with them in their taxi. We were supposed to have someone with Wasai to pick us up at the airport. I relent and decide to take a taxi since our people at Wasai had not yet showed up. As we were just about to leave the airport parking lot, we get waved at by another vehicle. It was the Wasai transportation. I told the taxi driver that I was sorry and had to go with them. I gave him a couple dollars for his trouble. The Wasai driver smoothed it over with him as well.

When we get to the lodge, the first thing they tell us is to go and pick out some rubber boots that fit. We did, and soon boarded our boat that was to take us into to the Tambopata Reserve. We would take the Madre de Dios River and the Tambopata. We travel about four hours upriver to our lodge. On the way they fed us some chicken and rice that were steamed in a big leaf. It was good and I ate every bit of it. We met a guy from Chico, California. He was going to be doing some volunteer work at the lodge in exchange for a discount on his lodging. Nice guy. Everything is made of wood. The main lodge has nice recliners to chill in while looking out at the jungle. Pretty freaking cool. We get to our lodge. It's an individual room with a porch facing the river. The humidity is massive. Our bed has a canopy with a net covering the whole bed. They told us to make sure to tuck the net in between the mattress and box spring. Just to keep the creepy crawlies from getting into your bed. Believe me there were plenty.

We had a catfish dinner. It was steamed in some bamboo. It was so good, and I had a beer. Ivan, our guide was a cool dude who had a good sense of humor. He knew so much. In our group was also this Jewish family from Israel. The husband, wife, and their daughter. She was probably in her early twenties. The father was a stereo-typical Jew. Always wanting to be first in line for everything and he treated his wife and daughter like shit. They prepared their own meals. The guides would prepare everyone else's food. After dinner, Ivan said, "Let's go take a walk in the jungle." Okay, everyone made their way out of the main lodge. I had a headlamp that as soon as I turned it on, I got bombarded by all these insects from every direction! I immediately took it off and held it in my hand. We started at the river's edge. We could see the caiman's glowing eyes in the water and there were some tapir tracks on the bank too. We headed into the jungle and Ivan pointed out a trap-door spider. It came out and practically greeted us. I saw its legs cock back just a bit. I backed off quickly. I didn't want that sucker jumping on me or anything! There were also some scorpions. On a tree was this red-headed bird called a "trogon." We returned to the lodge to get ready for bed. I decided to take a shower. No freaking hot water! It was cold as fuck! The coldest shower ever! And the shortest! It was unbearable and Ladema can attest to that. We also couldn't put paper in the toilet and had to put it in the waste paper basket. Ugh!

We would be leaving very early in the morning to a bird blind in the jungle. It's green everywhere! We make it to the blind after walking across the river on a fallen log. Ivan lets us know that there are four types of piranhas along with electric eels and stingrays. Okay, thanks for the warning. After taking some pictures we head on to a small village. I had an orange that someone gave me, and it was so sweet, so good. Later that day we would head on to the campsite in the jungle to be closer to the Macaw Clay Lick. We would have to leave very early to get there before the birds. We would wait for them in the blinds that they had. We would be sleeping in tents. When we got to the campsite there were ants everywhere! Ladema said, "Oh crap!" The ants sure were on a mission. Ivan said, "Oh they'll be gone in the morning." The guys fixed dinner for us and were friendly. I gave one of them my Timex Expedition watch with a green band and Ladema gave hers to someone as well.

After getting into our tents ready for bed, the Jewish guy, OMG! He snored so loud. It was extremely annoying. I felt like yelling for him to shut the fuck up! But I know I snore too. So, I just cut some serious farts and made Ladema and myself laugh out loud.

We left for the bird blind very early, it was still dark. I brought my Rebel with the zoom lens and a portable tripod. I also had the Canon camcorder. I could zoom in pretty good to get some cool shots. There were scarlet macaws and blue and gold macaws! They were beautiful! The guides said that the day before the birds didn't show up because there was this couple who had a child who was too loud and therefore, kept the birds away. We got lucky I guess and start heading back to the lodge around 9:30 A.M.

There at the lodge the guys there rescued a capuchin monkey who was being hunted by a harpy eagle. They have a string around his waist tied to a tree growing beside the lodge on the second floor.

I noticed him and tried to get him to come to me. I ask if he has a name, Martin, they say. He climbs on my shoulder and I offer him a raisin from my trail mix. He takes it and we're friends now. Ladema is so taken with the monkey. He climbs on her shoulder too. It's so cool! What an experience! I felt so lucky to be able to have such an interaction.

We thought that we were going to have a little break from all the climbing we did in the mountains, but we were sadly mistaken. Even though we would be at sea level so to speak, you still must climb up from the river to wherever it is that you are going. Buildings near the river are up high and away from the riverbank. It's the freaking Amazon! It floods!

Later that afternoon we walked around the grounds there at the Wasai Lodge. There were some ginger plants with red and yellow blossoms that looked so cool. We walked down a trail to where they had a zipline platform high up a tree. We climbed up and Ladema went first. I videoed her sailing through the jungle. I thought about filming my ride, but I just wanted to enjoy the ride without having to worry about dropping the camera. So freaking cool! Ziplining through the Amazon! They also had these wire bridges. One wire to step on and one to hold on to. Fuck that. I passed on the chance. I knew that it would take more effort than I was willing to expend. The Jewish guy jumped at the chance to be first, I had to watch. He struggled and stayed in one spot for quite a while. His wife and daughter also gave it a go. They struggled even more but didn't quit. There in Israel, everyone must serve in the military as part of their national education and duty. So, they were tough cookies!

We would be heading back to Puerto Maldonado for a final night before heading back to Cusco. When we get there, we check into our room there at the Wasai Lodge in town. We had signed up for a canopy walk tour, but we were so freaking tired that we canceled. The guy said but you already paid for it! I know, I know, I said. We'll just call it a donation. He was very disappointed, but damn we could barely walk. Later, a couple of girls that went on the canopy tour said that they got to meet Julia Louise Dreyfuss. Shit! Really? Oh well, wasn't meant to be, I guess. We did have one more tour left and that was to Lake Sandoval.

We drive a little ways and park. We walk a couple of miles on a muddy trail to the lake. It's an oxbow lake. It used to be part of a river, but it shifted and became landlocked. On the trail, we see a class of young students walking the trail. I took a picture of them. They gladly smiled and posed. Pretty cool that a teacher can take their class out into the jungle! We go out on the lake on a small boat. It's the Jewish family and us. While we were leaving the dock, we were going through thick jungle. I saw what I thought was a caiman in the water. Then, Ivan said, "No it's an anaconda!" I had my camcorder out and was trying to find it. It was sort of spooky going through the canal to get to the lake. Ivan said that two weeks prior a man had been doing some work in that canal area, cutting the overgrowth, and was attacked by an anaconda. It tore his arm up bad. It scared the shit out of Ladema and she wanted us to hurry up and get out of that canal! The Jewish guy told Ladema that maybe it liked white meat. It pissed her off! What an asshole.

Ivan rowed the boat to different parts of the lake. We saw some bats on a palm tree and I saw a Hoatzin bird. It looks very primitive and prehistoric. There were soft-shelled turtles sunning themselves on a log and a big black bird cooling off by spreading its wings. I wouldn't want to go swimming in the lake though. It looked kind of nasty.

We start heading back down the trail. I was able to see an elusive saddleback tamarin and a blue morpho butterfly. I was able to video the butterfly.

Back in Puerto Maldonado, Ladema and I walked around and went into some shops. Ivan took us for a ride around town in his trishaw. It was very cool. There were quite a few trishaws there in town. I gave him a $100 tip. I should have given him more. Earlier the Jewish guy asked me, "How much tip should I give?" I told him to give what your heart tells you. Typical.

We have one more night in Cusco. We had to go to the Casa Andina to pick up our backpack and stuff. We check in first at the San Blas Boutique Hotel, then proceed to pick up our luggage back at the Casa Andina Hotel. When we get back, we head on down the street to see the twelve-sided stone and the Incan wall of stone. We took some pictures. Earlier when we were in Cusco, the guide showed us two walls on opposite sides of the street. One he called Inca, the ones with perfectly cut stones, and the other he called Incapables, with shoddy workmanship. He said that the Conquistadores thought that the gold was hidden between the rocks, so they destroyed them, and then tried to put them back together, and did a piss-poor job at that!

As it turns out, everyone is celebrating Inti Raymi. In the San Blas neighborhood, there was a festival happening. Music, vendors, and people were everywhere. It was a cold evening, and I wore one of my Peruvian gorros. I bought a zampoña, one of those types of pan-flutes. It was a good, good time.

The following morning, we had to check out very early. The standard check-out time in Cusco is 8:00 A.M. No fucking joke! The flights arrive very early, so they need to have the rooms ready.

We head on out to have breakfast. At the hotel, they allowed us to leave our bags there a while. Our flight was leaving at 4:00 P.M. So, we go and have a big breakfast at some restaurant. I like the motifs and decorations that they had there, like some framed quipus on the wall. They are colorful bracelets with long knotted strings that the Incas used to communicate. We head on down to the Catedral. There were plenty of art students all around hustling their art. We bought a portrait of a child and some smaller prints. When we bought something from someone, they felt that I should buy one from them too. Sound familiar? Soon we head on to the airport and are back at home. What a trip!

25. Palau, Undersea Heaven

Palau! Wow! This could have been about Fiji or Bali, but Palau won out. This was to be the furthest that I have ever traveled away from home. This should have been a two-week vacay, but unfortunately it was only one. On the flight I ate supper four times before we made it to Palau. We had layovers in Hawaii, Guam, and Yap. Hawaii was only halfway to our destination! I would have liked to have stayed three nights in Yap to dive with the manta rays. The airport there in Yap was quite tiny. They did have a very large wood carving that showed some historical event. In their culture they used to use "stone money." Some of them were quite big. By the time we got to Palau, we had been on the plane for 25 hours! Not straight, which made it worse.

If you have never seen what Palau looks like, I recommend that you look it up online. Check out the islands and undersea life. It's difficult to put into words seeing it in person! When we get to Palau, the hotel sends a driver to pick us up at the airport, it was around 10:00 P.M. The driver turns around and looks at us with a smile and asks, "So, we go diving in the morning? I pick you up at 8:00, okay?" I said, "No, no way." We were exhausted. All I could think of was sleeping in a bed! I told him that we would go by the dive shop, Fish n Fins, in the early afternoon.

The next day we registered at the dive shop and gave them our info. For this trip we purchased dive insurance with DAN. I didn't want to be without insurance on the other side of the world. I told them that we were too tired to dive in the morning, and asked if we could dive the house reef, just outside. No problem. I wanted to see a mandarinfish. It's the reason that I came to Palau.

When my father was at the hospital in Corpus Christi, he was at Christus Spohn. In their waiting room downstairs, they have a salt-water aquarium. There, was this little colorful fish of green with orange stripes and a bit of blue around their mouths with some little yellow spots on the side below its jaw. It would come out and show itself. It would retract into the intricate coral trying to remain unseen. It was so beautiful! I looked up the fish and I remember saying to Ladema that I wanted to see it in its natural habitat. For me, it had to be Palau. I was given a five-pound weight tied to a long string and a float. This was to let boats know that there's a diver down. It's a bit murky, but I *did* catch a few glimpses of a mandarinfish. They come out near sundown and do a mating dance just above the coral they inhabit. There was some leaf coral all around. It was a so-so dive, a little too murky. We'll be able to see them a few days later at Mandarinfish Lake. I'm pretty sure it will be a much better dive than the house reef.

It's so convenient to be able to leave our gear at the dive shop. They had lockers that could accommodate all our gear. I did keep the cameras at the hotel. They also had a restaurant there by the dive shop. The restaurant had a good selection, but I wanted to try something different. At this point in our travels, we usually share a meal. The portions are huge and leave us feeling miserable after eating so much. Anyway, I order the raw tuna. It's thinly-sliced with some type of sauce and bread sticks. It's okay, I mean it really doesn't have a lot of flavor. Ladema has some but doesn't like it at all. We can't finish it and I feel a little bad about it. It doesn't last too long though. We ordered some soup back at the hotel. We saw a couple having some and it looked so good. So, I asked them what it was? I can't remember now, but it was some kind of Filipino soup. It was all Filipinos working at the hotel. They were very nice, and we had a good time talking with them.

We were staying at the Rose Garden Hotel. Our room was on the third level. Fuck, I had to carry all the gear up the flight of stairs our first night there. The hotel was made of very solid, probably mahogany wood. The hotel had a decent restaurant. The couple we met were living in the Philippines doing research with sharks. She called herself a "sharkologist." She was a marine biologist researching thresher sharks in combating cancer. They were on all our dives. Upon returning home, I did send her copies of my videos. Lots of sharks, yeah!

It's so cool, the dive shop comes to our hotel to pick us up! It's all part of the deal I guess? Anyway, we're diving with NITROX, everyone on our boat is. I'm so glad that we got certified before we got here. After our dives we didn't feel so tired like when using air. Checking my regulator, I noticed that it was slightly free-flowing. I took it inside the shop to get it checked out. I think it was the owner's son who looked at it. He was probably fourteen or fifteen. He fixed it in a jiffy, let's go dive!

Our first dive was Siaes Tunnel. We dove in and were fighting the current staying on top of the water trying not to float away. This was freaking tiring. Finally, everyone was ready to go down. I've got my camera rig ready to go! I had an alarm on my wrist computer set for 96 feet. It's dangerous to go too deep with NITROX. Suddenly, I check my depth gauge and I'm at 117 feet! Fuck! My alarm is going off, but I don't hear it. I get back up to where I need to be. We go on through the tunnel and on out. Ladema asked me later if I had not heard the alarm? Nope. We then dove Ulong Channel. This was our first reef hook experience. It's a Palauan thing. You hook onto a piece of rock or dead coral and pump a little air into your BC and you're floating, facing into the current, watching the parade of fish go by! I had my hands free to film the action. Oh boy, oh boy! This is too cool!

We find a spot to hook onto and see all these sharks everywhere and I'm filming it! What a rush! I stayed in the same spot for forty minutes! I just filmed all the sharks. There were around fifteen to twenty at any one time. I got some good close-ups! Our divemaster, Malsol, gave us the signal to "unhook," so we did. The current took us for one hell of a ride! I tried to film the stuff that I was swimming by, but the current was way too strong. I pointed the camera down as we were going over a big patch of lettuce coral. It was amazing! There were all kinds of other stuff too. Like, emperor angelfish, several types of sea anemone, clownfish, Moorish idols, Napoleon wrasse, moray eels, turtles, nudibranchs, lionfish, white-tip reef sharks, well, I could keep going and going. I could not believe all the different types of corals, all kinds! You had the hard and the soft corals. The soft corals were very colorful, but then so were the hard corals.

At the dive shop, we picked from a menu what we would have for lunch during our dive days. They would pack us our box lunches with a plastic water bottle filled tea. It had their logo. I thought that was a cool souvenir. On our first day we had barbeque chicken. Shit! I thought that I was back in Texas! Then I looked around, surrounded by rock islands in shallow turquoise water, nope. It was very good. After we had lunch, we still had some surface interval time to kill, so we went snorkeling. I'm so glad we did. We were in a spot where we could stand if we wanted and saw all these giant tridacna clams! They had all these different colors! We took a bunch of pics. That was so cool. I couldn't believe that we were here!

We did a dive on New Drop Off Reef. Let me tell you there were all these eels within the walls surrounded by colorful sponges and corals. It was so beautiful! I can't say that enough! I'm not exaggerating either.

The tides were very drastic there. The first day of diving everything was normal. The water level was just below the boat dock on the foundation. When we dove the house reef our first day the water was very low, and we had to climb down a ladder to get to it.

Another morning the tide was up and there was water way up on the foundation. I guess it's normal, but to me it looked like it had flooded. Am I back in Texas?

We met the owners of Fish-n-Fins. They were a very nice German couple. They gave us a private tour of one of their liveaboard boats. Now that's the way to go diving! There is so much freedom and ease to dive the best places. The ship was very comfortable. It had decent size quarters. It also had a huge camera table so that photographers and videographers could set up their rigs with ease. That would be one of my dreams, to go and do a liveaboard. Let me add that Fish n Fins has an excellent website that is very informative. It has information on the reefs, culture and pictures. Go to FishnFins.com

I had given Malsol a good tip and after that he catered to Ladema and me. I asked him if he could score some smoke, a couple of doobies or something. The next day he did bring a couple of big joints that I broke up and made four out of them. It was okay, nothing great or anything. There in Palau, people chew betelnut. They say it's very addicting. They use cigarette tobacco and put some of the betelnut mixed in with it and chew it. They spit red. The driver who drove us to the dive shop was complaining that there were stains in the vehicle.

On one of our dives, I was admiring the huge coral formations when a diver drops down and crashes on some of the coral. I'm fucking screaming at him and the divemaster chews him out. The diver was a young man traveling with his dad, they were Germans. They were really nice, but damn I wish people would control their buoyancy better. There's no telling how many years of coral was destroyed, hundreds? Probably thousands, sadly. We all stayed on the boat for a third dive around 5:00 P.M. We headed out to Mandarinfish Lake. It was not really a lake, but a protected little cove in shallow water. We had to swim a little way to get to the spot. They anchored the boat, and we were swimming with all this vegetation around us. It was a very cool area. On the way we see a huge crop of pink coral. Malsol said it was rare. We get to where there's a bunch of dead coral. Piles and piles of it. There's about ten yards or so of it. We're looking and looking for them. Malsol points one out to me. I start trying to capture it on video and film. I was using my JVC Piscio mini video camera and when I ran out of battery power, I used my Mini DVD camcorder and then the still camera. I hadn't had a chance to charge anything since we had not returned to our hotel. We headed back to the boat right around dusk. We were near the dive shop. Their boats have twin engines, and they haul ass! I like to sit in the back of the boat normally. On one trip Ladema and I had to sit up front. Oh my! It was a little rough. On one dive we did Virgin Blue Hole. When I did a back roll off the boat, I hit my head on the rock roof that was just beneath the boat. I went into one of the holes and then descended. Malsol told me that he would point out what they call the "disco clam." It was in a wall and was about three or four inches wide. It was white with red tentacles around the edges. When it would open you could see what looked like a flash of electricity shoot across on the inside of the clam. It looked very cool. We got to dive Blue Corner twice! The currents had to be just right to dive there. When we finally got down, we hooked on. Malsol helped Ladema with her hook. I had some awesome footage! The sharks swam up very close to me, which was fine. They had gotten a little too close for comfort for Ladema and she signaled Malsol, to move her the fuck back! She made sure to tell me to get her in the shot with some sharks and I did. She has come a long way to do something like this. Not too many people are eager to dive with sharks. I never felt a bit threatened. Palau was the first shark sanctuary in the world. Besides the sharks there are these huge shoals of all kinds of fish! I'm so glad that we got to come to Palau!

For lunch one day we went to a small island. It had picnic tables and there were many palm trees all around. We had to find a restroom. The crew brought us our boxed lunches. It was good as usual whatever we had. As we were there eating lunch I thought, *Wow! If this had been some seventy years ago, our countries would have been at war.* There was Ladema and I representing the U.S., the Germans, a Japanese instructor, a guy from New Zealand, a Swiss couple, and French guy. Well, except for the Swiss couple we wouldn't have been able to sit at the table together. How weird, ¿no?

It was the island where Jellyfish Lake is. You have a little hiking to do. I really would have liked to do it, however the sharkologist and her boyfriend told us that when they had gone earlier in the week, there were blacktip sharks you could check out while snorkeling. Besides, the Jellyfish Lake Tour would have been $25 each, the sharks were free. So that's what I did. I had my mini video recorder and sure enough the blacktips showed up. They were sort of playing in the sand with each other. I guess they could have been hunting something. It was so cool! There were other colorful little fish. I think I saw what was a humuhumunukunukuapua'a, the Hawaiian State Fish. It' a type of triggerfish. I stayed there watching the blacktips play. They came and checked me out. They saw that it was only a Chicano and quickly resumed their play. I didn't feel at all threatened. Ladema was chilling on the beach having a smoke. She did feel uncomfortable with the sharks.

We dove German Channel hoping to see some manta rays. We went down and had to crouch and hide and wait for them to show up. After a while nothing. We moved a little way down to find a new spot and I see a manta about seventy feet away and was able to get it on video. It seemed to be hauling ass. When we got back on the boat, some of the divers had seen a hammerhead. I'm sure the manta was trying to stay away from it. I wish that I could have the seen hammerhead! Oh well what you gonna do?

On our way back to the dive shop I bring out the beef jerky and pass it around. Everyone takes some. It was so good! Everyone was so cool. Couldn't have asked for a better group of people to dive with!

On one of our days that we didn't dive we rented a car and drove around Koror and went into some shops and a shopping center. We bought some t-shirts and souvenirs. We then took a long drive out into the countryside and drove by the Palauan version of our White House. It was a big white house where the president of Palau lives. There didn't seem to be much security. I didn't want to get in trouble and turned around and headed back to the hotel. On the side of the road were these workers who were cutting the grass with a machete! That's a lot of labor.

It was evening and time to go, our plane was to leave at 10:00 P.M. We got a ride from the hotel to the airport. About five of the women working there at the hotel accompanied us. They really took a liking to Ladema and me. We hugged and took pictures and cried. Good, good people. Our return flight to Texas would take us to Japan then fly direct to Houston. Our short layover at the Narita airport in Japan was very cool. It was very modern. It even had an indoor smoking room with excellent ventilation. Ladema liked that. Soon we were on our way back to Houston. Awesome, awesome trip!

It is now the summer of 2021, and the U.S. has opened. I don't think it will be safe to travel internationally just yet. I will be waiting for the granddaughters to get vaccinated, they are ten and eleven. I hope that there will be a vaccine at the end of this summer or by the fall. But there's something I like even more than traveling, and that is living in a democracy. Ours right now is in peril, you know that! Help protect it by voting blue no matter who! Be safe, be excellent to each other and be curious about the world we live in.

ABOUT THE AUTHOR

Sonny currently lives in Kyle, Texas, with his wife Ladema and two granddaughters, Holly and Audrey, along with his stepson Barry and their four cats, Slick Willie, Dottie, Frankie, and Sharky. He spends his morning watching The Stephanie Miller and Thom Hartmann Show on Free Speech TV, working in his yard, reading, and playing guitar. He has been unemployed since his retirement from teaching in 2017. He was diagnosed with hereditary photoreceptor dystrophy, a type of retinitis pigmentosa in 2015 and his vision has deteriorated since then. He is deaf and was also diagnosed with Sarcoidosis, an auto-immune condition in 2019. He is legally blind. He is working on his second book about his teaching career and experiences.

ADDENDUM

Dale Smith found my book online and made contact with me through someone I knew. We had an excellent conversation that lasted a few days. He let me know what was going on in his head during our time at Playa Ziplite in Puerto Angel.

Everyone had eaten some mushrooms, but Dale ate quite a bit more than anyone, so he was tripping pretty hard. We were surrounded by the Marineros, the Federal police beach patrol. Dale saw me walk away with the head officer. I thought that I was going to throw up and squatted, then went down on my knees since I was a little dizzy. Dale in the meantime saw this and thought that we were all going to be killed on the beach. He hadn't even told his folks where he was going to be. He told Rafael that he thought he was going to faint, saying "I can't watch this, I can't watch this" then he passed out. He said he felt one of the soldiers tapping his head with his boot or gun stock. All the while stating to himself, "I can't feel this, I can't feel this!... This had been too much for Dale, Rafael, and Clay and they went straight to bed. After nearly forty years Dale Smith, a friend and former student, was found.